The Grapes of Wrath
and 24 More Videos

Activities for High School English Classes

Randy Larson

J. Weston Walch, Publisher

Portland, Maine

User's Guide
to
Walch Reproducible Books

As part of our general effort to provide educational materials which are as practical and economical as possible, we have designated this publication a "reproducible book." The designation means that purchase of the book includes purchase of the right to limited reproduction of all pages on which this symbol appears:

Here is the basic Walch policy: We grant to individual purchasers of this book the right to make sufficient copies of reproducible pages for use by all students of a single teacher. This permission is limited to a single teacher, and does not apply to entire schools or school systems, so institutions purchasing the book should pass the permission on to a single teacher. Copying of the book or its parts for resale is prohibited.

Any questions regarding this policy or requests to purchase further reproduction rights should be addressed to:

Permissions Editor
J. Weston Walch, Publisher
321 Valley Street • P. O. Box 658
Portland, Maine 04104-0658

—J. Weston Walch, Publisher

On the cover: still from The Grapes of Wrath © *1993 Everett Collection, Inc.*

1   2   3   4   5   6   7   8   9   10

ISBN 0-8251-2448-4

Contents

To the Teacher

I remember sitting in science class in junior high and getting excited as the lights dimmed and the movie projector began to chatter. A grandfatherly scientist from Bell Laboratories loomed large on the three-legged screen and began to tell about the neat workings of our universe and the role that the sun played in it all. When it was over, someone snapped on the light, shut off the projector, and totally shattered the dream. I remember looking around, while I collected my books, at all the sad and lonely friends of Mr. Sun who had to get ready for Phys. Ed. within a few minutes of the next bell. It was a shock that I felt deeply, and could do nothing about—until now.

I've written this book because I've learned that shutting off a video machine doesn't shut off the emotions and imaginings of the audience, and that the best opportunity for teaching is right after the words THE END appear; it's where real learning can start, if we know how to seize the moment. The activities included in this text give you some effective ways to move kids from the world they've encountered on film to the realities of curriculum requirements in the classroom. I've included essays, projects, speeches, interviews, self-studies, word games, multiple choice and true/false quizzes, vocabulary exercises, and more, in order to bring variety to the task of learning from film. By using the teaching tips listed on the following page, and by selecting exercises appropriate to students of various ability levels, you can help create a meaningful experience for every student.

There are many good English teachers who resist this experience out of hand. Their position is that too much time is already spent by today's youth in front of a television screen. Why provide even more viewing time in school? For those earnest souls I offer the following evidence on behalf of video use in the English/Language Arts classroom:

- First—Let's be practical. Videos are cheap. A classroom set of novels might run $90 to $180,

while a video costs $2 to $4 to rent. If you're short of funds, videos are one answer.

- Second—Videos are time-savers. You can show a video in three days, while a novel may take three weeks. In a packed curriculum, videos allow time to teach more skills at a greater depth.

- Third—Videos provide a springboard into all sorts of other genres and media—poetry, plays, essays, biographies, novels, screenplays, research, and journalism. After a video many students ask for more; I immediately suggest a book, a poem, an essay, or a news feature that expands on the topic or relates to the film in some important way.

- Fourth—Videos are democratic in their range and depth. All students can get to the core of most films, not just the literati who are sensitive to the rhythm and nuance of language. This makes for more inclusive class discussions and more success on written assignments.

- Fifth—Videos provide variety. In a curriculum that looks dolefully out upon 180 days of school, one must reach for new ways to teach kids. Videos can be a handy solution to the doldrums.

- Finally—Videos are powerful expressions of great artists' and directors' visions. They bring a dimension to a piece of literature that cannot be found on the stage or in a book. Since it is an English teacher's task to make as many literary experiences available to kids as possible, videos should be used in the classroom whenever the opportunity strikes.

And there's one more reason for teaching literature through videos—this book. The many activities within its covers give you a wide range of exercises to offer students in this engaging approach to the study of literature. It is my hope that by using this text, my colleagues will be better able to give students what can be rightfully called a good education.

Teaching Tips

Preview, Preview, Preview

The films in this book were chosen to include a wide range of interests, abilities, and school climates. Some contain nudity and profanity. Others contain suggestive scenes that you may not want your students to see. *Preview* each film before showing to determine whether the film is appropriate for your classes.

Choose Wisely

Finding the right film for the right group of students is critical. If the film is too complex for your students, you could spend more time stopping horseplay than anything else. If the video is too simplistic for your students, boredom wins out and the exercise is a disaster. The best way to solve this problem is to imagine the average student from a particular class watching the film with you as you preview it. Try to internalize his or her reaction to the dialogue, action (or lack of it), theme, and tone of the film.

Prepare the Way

Read the plot summary provided here and preview the film; then make a few notes about key points or scenes that you want the students to notice. Bypass the credits and start the tape with the action. Set the tape counter to zero and keep track of where you finish for that day on a 3-by-5 card for each class. Set the VCR in a convenient place for optimum viewing by all students, preferably up on a stand or cart at the front of the room.

Stop Often—Lights On!

Pause the film whenever you need to make a brief, important point, and turn the lights on if you feel it will help the students focus their attention. In fact, some teachers keep the lights on during the entire film. Have short discussions as the movie progresses. Even a short quiz would work in some cases.

Quit Early

Try not to end a tape when the bell rings. Shutting things down about 10–15 minutes before class ends gives you a chance to hold a brief discussion on one or two major points in the film. Letting the students drift out the door as the bell rings gives them 24 hours to forget what they saw.

Make a Viewing Guide

Jot down some key points and questions about scenes from the film on slips of paper and photocopy them for the students' reference as the tape rolls. They will be more apt to stay "on task" if they have to respond, even if briefly in one-word answers, to some short, to-the-point questions.

Subscribe

One of the best publication aids for teachers using video in their classes is: *Learning Enrichment* published by Learning Enrichment, Inc., Grand Central Station, P.O. Box 5530, New York, NY 10163-5530. This newsletter/magazine gives tips on how to use television and video more effectively in the classroom; explains the "fair use" laws for teachers who want to tape certain programs off the major networks for use in the classroom; and lists "coming attractions" (movies, shows, news programs, specials) that might appeal to teachers of all disciplines.

THE GRAPES OF WRATH

Author: John Steinbeck

Novel Title: *The Grapes of Wrath*

Director: John Ford

Running Time: 129 minutes

Year: 1940

Format: black and white

Summary

Tom Joad, the oldest son of a poor Oklahoma farm family, has just been released on parole for killing a man in a drunken brawl. He's walking the familiar road to home when he meets the local ex-preacher, Casy, who has been defrocked for debauching young girls who came to him for comfort. Casy and Tom go to Tom's home, only to find it abandoned. A half-crazed neighbor named Muley Graves comes out of hiding to tell Tom the story of the Joads' ejection by company men who hired bulldozers to shove them off their land.

The next day Tom finds his family at his Uncle John's place. They all load their belongings into a worn-out farm truck, and all 12 travelers, including Casy, head for California. Before they reach California, Granma and Grampa Joad die and are buried along the road. The Joads travel on to a migrant pickers' camp where the children are starving and the men are desperate for work. When a contractor pulls in offering work, a man in the crowd challenges him to put his price-per-box in writing. The contractor tells the sheriff to arrest the man as an "agitator." The man punches the sheriff and runs. The sheriff shoots and kills a woman bystander and, as he is about to shoot again, Tom and Casy tackle him and knock him out. Since Tom is on parole, Casy tells him to hide and Casy takes the blame.

Threatened with the camp being "burned out," the Joads take to the road again and end up at the Keene Ranch picking peaches. To get in they have to break a strikers' line under armed guard. After supper, Tom sneaks out of camp to see what the trouble is and finds Casy and some of the strikers down by the river. When the camp guards come, Tom and the men are attacked as they try to slip away, and Casy is clubbed to death. Tom strikes out, kills one of the attackers, and runs off.

After hiding Tom under blankets in the truck, Tom's family leaves camp. They drive until they run out of gas, then coast into a camp run by the Department of Agriculture. The committee-run camp is clean and decent and Tom and some of the men find work at a nearby farm. One day the farm owner confides to them that some town toughs are planning to start a fight during the camp's Saturday-night dance. If this were to happen, the sheriff and his men would raid the camp and shut it down because of rioting. On the night of the dance, camp people subdue the ruffians just as the sheriff and his men show up. With no cause to enter the camp, the sheriff must turn back, and the camp is saved.

Soon after, the police come to the camp suspecting Tom Joad is there. They say he's wanted for murder and they will bring a search warrant with them next time. Tom decides to run, but before he goes his mother stops him and says good-bye. Tom tell his mother that he must try to find out what's going on, what's wrong with things. He's going to give his life for the cause of feeding the poor and helping the downtrodden. Ma Joad kisses Tom, and he slips off into the night.

The next day the family leaves Wheat Patch Camp and heads for Fresno to pick cotton. "We're the people that live. We'll go on forever, 'cause we're the people," Ma Joad says, and the truck rolls on down the road on its journey west.

Name _____ Date _____

The Grapes of Wrath

Multiple Choice

Write the letter of the correct answer to each item on the line provided.

1. _____ In the opening scene, Tom Joad is walking home from: (a) college (b) the city (c) prison (d) the army

2. _____ Casy, the ex-preacher, doesn't preach anymore because: (a) he was thrown out of church (b) he killed a man (c) he drinks alcohol (d) he doesn't have anything to preach about

3. _____ Tom Joad comes home to find: (a) Muley Graves hiding in the Joad family's empty house (b) the entire family hiding at Uncle Charlie's (c) a crazy man hiding in the cellar with a gun (d) a preacher with a bottle of corn whiskey (e) a and b (f) b and c

4. _____ The Joad family heads to California because: (a) the bank has repossessed their farm (b) they are starving (c) they need a place to call "home" (d) handbills have promised lots of work and high wages (e) a and b (f) a and c (g) a, b, and c (h) a, b, c, and d (i) none of the above

5. _____ What does California symbolize to the Joad family? (a) paradise (b) security (c) escape (d) God (e) a and b (f) a and c (g) a, b, and c (h) a, b, and d

6. _____ The Joads find out about the hardships awaiting them in California by: (a) reading yellow hand-bills (b) listening to news reports on the radio (c) listening to neighbors talk (d) listening to a man tell of his children who starved to death (e) a and d

7. _____ When the Joads first get to California they have to park in a "camp" which is: (a) a collection of families waiting to find jobs (b) a park run by the California Fruit Growers Association (c) a social organization run by the Fruit Pickers Union (d) a and b

8. _____ The fruit pickers are on "strike," which means: (a) they're too lazy to work (b) they're too weak to work (c) they won't work until the wages go up (d) b and c

9. _____ The roughnecks want to start a fight at the government camp because: (a) then the sheriff will have a legal excuse to come on the property and arrest people (b) the fruit pickers will see the power of the growers' association and give up the strike (c) they like the chance to fight when the odds are in their favor

10. _____ Tom kills a man outside of the Keene Ranch because: (a) he lost his temper (b) the man killed Casy (c) he wasn't thinking; he was reacting (d) he went insane (e) a and b (f) b and c (g) a, b, and c (h) a, b, c, and d (i) none of the above

11. _____ Tom has to leave the government camp because: (a) the sheriff is about to find him and arrest him for murder (b) Casy's teachings have prodded him to go out and find the "truth" (c) the law will follow his family as long as they think Tom is with them (d) a and b (e) a, b, and c

12. _____ Just before he leaves, Tom: (a) kisses his father (b) tells his mother he'll be back (c) tells his mother that she'll see him wherever injustice is being fought (d) gives his mother a necklace (e) a and b (f) a and c (g) a, b, and c (h) a, b, c, and d (i) none of the above

The Grapes of Wrath

Vocabulary

Below are ten terms used in the movie *The Grapes of Wrath*. Read the definitions and then write a brief summary of the movie, using at least seven of the terms. Underline the terms as you use them in the summary.

1. **touched**—slang for mentally unbalanced

2. **handbill**—a paper flyer containing newsworthy information

3. **parole**—conditional release of a prisoner before full sentence is served

4. **Okies**—people who left Oklahoma for California during the Depression

5. **Dust Bowl**—area in the central United States that lost its crops and topsoil because of drought and high winds during the 1930's

6. **contractor**—person who hires people for a job for a set price

7. **sharecropper**—person who farms someone's land for a share of the crops

8. **dogs**—a slang term meaning someone's feet

9. **cats**—a shortened term that refers to the machines built by the Caterpillar Tractor Company

10. **Red**—someone who believes in a communistic socialistic form of government, as many did during the 1930's when capitalism seemed to have failed as a valid economic system

_____
_____
_____
_____
_____
_____
_____
_____
_____
_____
_____
_____
_____
_____
_____
_____
_____

Name _____ Date _____

The Grapes of Wrath

Dialogue

Dialogue is what people say to each other—the exact words they speak. In *The Grapes of Wrath* many lines spoken by the characters are in the language of the farmers and field workers from the Oklahoma prairie. The language contains slang, colloquialisms, and similes that carry important meaning.

Read the lines below spoken by some of the characters in *The Grapes of Wrath*. Then, on the lines provided, explain what each speaker meant.

1. Tom, to truck driver who gave him a ride: "I'd a-walked it, but my dogs is pooped."

   _____

   _____

2. Muley, to Tom and Casy at Tom's parents' farm: "Listen. The wind's fixin' to do something."

   _____

   _____

3. Bulldozer driver, to Muley before he crushes Muley's house: "What happens to other folks is their own look-out."

   _____

   _____

4. Tom, to his mother before setting out for California: "Are we goin' to California true?"

   _____

   _____

5. Ma Joad, to Tom when Tom is contemplating leaving: "Pa's lost his place. He ain't the head no more."

   _____

   _____

6. Tom, to his mother just before he leaves: "Casy was like a lantern."

   _____

   _____

7. Ma, to Pa Joad after Tom has gone and the family is moving on: "It's all in one flow like a stream."

   _____

   _____

The Grapes of Wrath

Essay

Below are the first lines of "The Battle Hymn of the Republic," from which John Steinbeck took the phrase "grapes of wrath" for the title of his book. Think about how the concept of abundance applies to grapes, which grow in clusters and are so sweet, succulent, and beautiful when hanging on the vine. Then think about the second half of this famous phrase.

Write a short essay in which you discuss the full meaning of the title of this movie in terms of the life of the Joad family. What did they find in California? What did they expect to find? What did California symbolize for them? What truth did each one learn (Tom, Ma, Pa, Casy)?

Mine eyes have seen the glory of the coming of the Lord,
He is trampling out the vintage where the grapes of wrath are stored.
He hath loosed the fateful lightning of his terrible swift sword,
His truth is marching on.

_____

_____

_____

_____

_____

_____

_____

_____

_____

_____

_____

_____

_____

_____

_____

_____

_____

_____

_____

_____

_____

_____

_____

The Grapes of Wrath

Answers

Multiple Choice

1. c	7. a
2. d	8. c
3. a	9. a
4. h	10. g
5. g	11. e
6. d	12. g

Vocabulary

Sample answer:

Tom Joad, son of an Oklahoma <u>sharecropper</u>, is out on <u>parole</u> for killing a man. He finds his family gone from home and a neighbor, Muley Graves, hiding out like a criminal inside the house. Muley appears to be <u>touched</u> but the preacher, Casy, assures him that he's sane. Muley tells of how the <u>cats</u> came and smashed down his house and drove him off the land. He tells of how the <u>Dust Bowl</u> has finally blown the land, the crops, and now the people away. Tom's family, after reading a <u>handbill</u>, sets out with thousands of families called <u>Okies</u> to find work and security and paradise in the great and distant state of California.

Dialogue

1. Tom's feet (dogs) are tired and he can't walk much farther.

2. The wind is about to start blowing; it's getting ready to blow up a storm.

3. People have to fend for themselves, to look after their own affairs.

4. Are we really going to California?

5. Your father isn't the leader of the family anymore; he can't make any important decisions because he's lost his desire to take on new challenges.

6. Casy (the preacher) turned on the light of new ideas, new thoughts in Tom's mind; this allowed Tom to "see" and understand the real issues facing poor people across the country.

7. Life is a continuous flow of events, one running into and mixing with another—not a series of abrupt, unrelated moments with no purpose or direction.

Essay

Essays will vary.

THE MAN WHO WOULD BE KING

Author: Rudyard Kipling
Short Story Title: "The Man Who Would Be King"
Director: John Huston

Running Time: 129 minutes
Year: 1975
Format: color

Summary

Peachey Carnehan, an ex-soldier from the British army, stumbles into the office of the *Northern Star* run by a man named Kipling and begins the story of how he and his friend, Danny Dravot, ventured into the land of Kafiristan to become kings.

The scene flashes back to a moment, three years before, when Peachey is "lifting" Kipling's watch at a railroad station. Realizing he's robbed a "brother" Freemason, Peachey returns the watch, thereby striking up a friendship. Soon after, Peachey and Danny ask Kipling to witness a contract between them that describes certain behaviors that each must adhere to in achieving their latest objective—to be kings of Kafiristan. Kipling witnesses the document, bestows the Masonic medallion upon Danny for good luck, and the two leave for the "land of opportunity."

While in the mountains above Kafiristan, Danny and Peachey, finding themselves unable to cross a great crevasse, sit by a fire and laugh as old memories come to mind. Their laughter quickly causes an avalanche which fills the crevasse and allows them to enter into the "promised land." Once there, they meet Billy Fish, an English rifleman left over from a failed geographical expedition. Billy interprets for Danny and Peachey during their stay in Kafiristan and makes introductions for them to the king of the Er-Heb, a bald coward named Ootah.

Danny and Peachey train the Er-Hebites in fighting tactics, conquer the Bashkai people, and form a huge army with which they conquer all of Kafiristan. During the first battle Danny is struck by an arrow that lodges in his bandolier and does him no harm. The Bashkai declare Danny a god, the son of Secanda I, the first conquering "god" who came in 328 B.C. (actually, Alexander the Great). Danny wants no part of it, but Peachey talks him into accepting the position.

One day the high priest calls on Danny to come to Secandagal to prove his worthiness as a god.

Danny and Peachey go, but without the army. The high priest draws a sword and is about to split Danny's chest in half, when he spies the Masonic medallion hanging from a chain around his neck. He bows, and the people submit to Danny as a true god because Alexander the Great (Secanda I) carved a Masonic emblem on a rock in the temple to leave as his sign.

In the temple, Danny and Peachey find a vast store of gold and jewels, but must wait four months until the weather will allow them to leave with the riches. As the months pass, Danny becomes convinced that he truly is the rightful king of Kafiristan. "You should bow before me like the others," he tells Peachey. Peachey is alarmed, but is not shaken until Danny announces that he intends to stay and marry a woman named Roxanne so he will have heirs to the throne. But the priests resist Danny because any woman taken by a god will burst into a pillar of fire the moment she is touched. Danny insists on proceeding with the marriage and asks Peachey to stay for the wedding. At the ceremony Peachey stands by while a fearful Roxanne is brought before Danny, Secanda II. Roxanne bites Danny's cheek and draws blood. The high priest declares Danny's humanity and the people chase Danny and Peachey to the edge of the city where Danny is catapulted off the bridge he had built across a great chasm. Peachey is crucified but released when he doesn't die.

The film ends as Peachey presents Kipling with Danny's skull, which he has carried with him during his year-long trip out of Kafiristan. "He became the king of Kafiristan and wore a crown on his head, and that's all there is to tell." Peachey leaves Kipling in his office with the head of his beloved friend saying, "I've got business in the South. I have to meet a man at Malabar Junction." The camera closes in on the skull and the crown; the film ends.

The Man Who Would Be King

Multiple Choice

Write the letter of the correct answer to each item on the line provided.

1. _____ Peachey Carnehan and Danny Dravot are ex-: (a) sailors (b) soldiers (c) convicts

2. _____ Which saying best describes their view of life? (a) "A stitch in time saves nine" (b) "No man is an island" (c) "Eat, drink, and be merry, for tomorrow you may die"

3. _____ The strange thing about Peachey's narration of the story is that: (a) he talks about himself in the third person (b) he makes the events more exciting than they really were (c) he doesn't tell Kipling the whole story (d) he's talking from the grave (e) b and c

4. _____ If Peachey had stolen someone else's watch he and Danny would have: (a) ended up rich men (b) been arrested for vagrancy (c) come back much sooner (d) been murdered by the high priest in Secandagal (e) b and d (f) a and c (g) a, b, and c (h) none of the above

5. _____ Peachey and Danny signed a contract to: (a) become gods of the lower Ganges Region (b) become gods to the high priests of Kafiristan (c) become kings of Kafiristan (d) bring enlightenment to the darker regions of the earth (e) a and b (f) a, b, and c

6. _____ The trouble starts when: (a) Danny decides to become king (b) Peachey says he'll stay to watch Danny get married to Roxanne (c) Peachey talks Danny into becoming Secanda II (d) Danny is shot with an arrow that sticks harmlessly into his leather bandolier

7. _____ Peachey tells Danny to accept the title of the god, Secanda II, because: (a) it'll please the people (b) it'll please Billy Fish (c) it'll be easier to loot the country (d) if they don't, the people will slay them like beggars (e) no one will believe them back in India

8. _____ Danny is officially declared a god when: (a) the high priest can't kill him (b) Roxanne falls at his feet in awe (c) the high priest recognizes the Masonic medallion hanging from Danny's neck (d) Danny declares he will stay in Kafiristan and rule the people

9. _____ Danny decides to stay on as Secanda II rather than leave with the gold because he: (a) believes he truly is the king of Kafiristan (b) realizes he can do some good as king of Kafiristan (c) wants Roxanne as his wife (d) wants to leave an heir to follow him on the throne

10. _____ Danny and Peachey would have been able to complete the terms of their contract if: (a) Danny had not taken himself so seriously (b) Danny had refused the title of Secanda II (c) Danny had not decided to marry Roxanne (d) a and b (e) a, b, and c (f) a and c (g) none of the above

11. _____ The major force operating in this film is: (a) providence (b) fate (c) evil (d) coincidence (e) gravity (f) stupidity

12. _____ The main theme in the film is: (a) in playing God, man destroys himself (b) ignorance is man's greatest weapon (c) primitive man controls his destiny, while modern man only influences it (d) man's lust for power is a dangerous tool in the hands of kings

The Man Who Would Be King

Cause and Effect

An interesting plot is made of events that logically grow out of one another; because event A happens, event B must follow. In this pattern we would say that event A was the *cause* and event B was the *effect*, or result. Then event B causes the effect of event C, and C causes D, and so forth.

Below are several cause events. Write out the effect(s) of those events in the space provided. Some events may produce more than one effect.

1. Peachey steals Kipling's watch.

   _____

   _____

2. Peachey and Danny reminisce and laugh at old memories while waiting to die.

   _____

   _____

3. An arrow sticks into Danny's bandolier, leaving him unharmed.

   _____

   _____

4. Alexander the Great carved the symbol of the Freemasons on a rock in the temple at Secandagal.

   _____

   _____

5. Danny decides to stay and be king of Kafiristan.

   _____

   _____

6. Danny decides to marry Roxanne.

   _____

   _____

7. Roxanne bites Danny's cheek.

   _____

   _____

8. Peachey is crucified, then released.

   _____

   _____

The Man Who Would Be King

Verbs

Think of the title of Rudyard Kipling's story "The Man Who Would Be King" as the first part of a sentence that needs completing. This part of the sentence (the subject) includes the noun *man* and the adjective clause *who would be king*.

Complete the partial sentences below by adding words that tell something about the subject of the film. For example, in sentence 8 you might write, "The man who would be king is in for some serious surprises, some of them downright nasty."

1. The man who would be king **should**...

_____

_____

2. The man who would be king **might**...

_____

_____

3. The man who would be king **can't**...

_____

_____

4. The man who would be king **has**...

_____

_____

5. The man who would be king **must**...

_____

_____

6. The man who would be king **will**...

_____

_____

7. The man who would be king **could**...

_____

_____

8. The man who would be king **is**...

_____

_____

The Man Who Would Be King

Satire and Irony

Either describe what is being satirized, or explain the irony in each of the sentences below taken from "The Man Who Would Be King." Remember that satire is an attack on social customs, morals, or actions that the author sees as unjust or wicked, while irony is a statement or situation in which the intended meaning is the opposite of what is actually being said or done. Satire and irony are often couched in humor to give the message more sting.

1. When Peachey meets Ootah, king of the Er-Hebite people, he says, "We are not gods, but Englishmen, which is the next best thing."

   _____

   _____

2. Billy Fish has been telling Ootah about the habits of the English soldiers (giving names to dogs and taking hats off to women), and Danny says, "Bringing enlightenment to the darker regions of the world."

   _____

   _____

3. When Danny and Peachey are training the Er-Hebites to be soldiers, Danny says: "When we're done with you you'll be able to stand up and slaughter your enemies like civilized men."

   _____

   _____

4. Peachey describes Kafiristan to Kipling as "a land of warring tribes—that is, a land of opportunity…"

   _____

   _____

5. The Er-Hebites are playing polo using a man's head for a ball, and Danny becomes offended. Peachey says, "Mustn't be prejudiced, Danny. Different lands, different customs."

   _____

   _____

6. Danny and Peachey make out a formal contract between them that states in formal terms how they are to behave during their quest to become kings.

   _____

   _____

7. Peachey says to Billy Fish, "Now if you'll take us to this Ootah bloke, we'll begin his education."

   _____

   _____

The Man Who Would Be King

Answers

Multiple Choice

1. b	7. c
2. c	8. c
3. a	9. a
4. d	10. e
5. c	11. d
6. d	12. a

Cause and Effect

1. (a) They are brought before the district commissioner. (b) Danny is given the Masonic medallion.
2. The avalanche fills the crevasse.
3. He is declared a god by the Bashkai.
4. (a) Danny and Peachey are not killed by the high priest. (b) Danny is allowed to rule as Secanda II.
5. (a) Peachey decides to leave without Danny. (b) Danny passes 30-plus proclamations which makes him feel necessary to the people.
6. (a) The priests are angry with Danny. (b) The high priests sacrifice children and animals to appease the god called Imbra.
7. (a) Danny is killed. (b) Billy Fish is killed.
8. Peachey goes mad and carried Danny's head back to the modern world.

Verbs

Possible responses:

1. should prepare for the worst regardless of how the situation looks at first.
2. might wish the idea had never come to mind.
3. can't hope to succeed if the people revolt.
4. has the opportunity to experience absolute power, and its corrupting influence.
5. must not become enamored of the authority invested in the office.
6. will always feel alone and above everyone else.
7. could be very successful if he used common sense.
8. is a person with a great need to be important.

Satire and Irony

Possible responses:

1. Peachey is spouting the proud egocentric words of a person and a culture that feel far superior to anyone considered even remotely primitive, much as the entire Western world does. Since Peachey and Danny are the next best thing to gods, the Er-Hebites should be honored and happy to serve them in their enterprise.

2. Danny is comparing what they're doing to what missionaries have been blamed for: teaching other cultures to be Western, often with violent and disastrous results for all concerned.

3. Danny is talking as if there really is an accepted civilized way to kill other humans. Kipling is sneering at our belief that people killed "properly" are killed justly.

4. "Opportunity" is a term used in legitimate business discussions. By using this term Danny is scorning the moral world and setting up his own illegal, violent definition of the term.

5. Peachey is mocking the tourist mentality of many Western intruders who have ventured into foreign lands and made their stuffy pronouncements, even as they stood ready to exploit that same country and spoil it.

6. By formalizing their silly, exploitive adventure, Danny and Peachey are laughing at the whole legitimate world that conducts real business with real "legal" documents. They seem to be scorning the fact that many people and governments believe that as long as it's on a piece of paper the proclamation is moral, legal, and right.

GREAT EXPECTATIONS

Author: Charles Dickens
Novel Title: *Great Expectations*
Director: Kevin Connor

Running Time: 310 minutes
Year: 1989
Format: color

Summary

A small boy named Philip Pirrip, called Pip, is accosted on the marshes near his home by a convict on the run. At the convict's request, the boy brings him some food and a file and sets into motion the events that will alter the boy's life forever.

Little Pip lives in Kent with his cranky sister, Mrs. Joe, and her husband Joe Gargery, a blacksmith. He loves Joe but becomes dissatisfied with the "common" life at the forge after being hired by a rich, tormented lady, Miss Havisham, to play with her niece, Estella. Estella berates Pip, who leaves feeling ashamed, overwhelmed, and infatuated with her.

Years later, while Pip is apprenticed to Joe, a lawyer named Jaggers shows up in Kent with a proposition: Pip is to go to London and live as a gentleman, but he cannot inquire about his benefactor. Believing his benefactor is Miss Havisham, Pip gladly leaves the forge.

Pip's roommate in London is Herbert Pocket, who also has great expectations but can't seem to connect with the right business deal. Upon coming of age Pip receives 500 pounds from his benefactor through Jaggers. He contrives with Wemmick, Jaggers' assistant (a decent, caring fellow), to set Herbert up with a partnership in an accounting firm. Herbert is overjoyed that his expectations have come true.

The mood is shattered, however, when the convict whom Pip had helped as a child shows up to announce himself as Pip's secret benefactor. Pip is horrified! Neither Miss Havisham nor Estella has had anything to do with his fortune. The convict, Magwitch (alias Provis), had been exiled to Australia and is staying in London under penalty of death if discovered. Pip and Herbert plan an escape for Magwitch, but a criminal named Compeyson and his accomplice, Orlick (Joe Gargery's former apprentice who murdered Mrs. Joe and got away with it), watch Pip's apartment daily.

To profess his love to Estella, Pip goes to see Miss Havisham, who tells him the story of Estella's arrival at Satis House: She was three years old and smiling in her sleep when Jaggers carried her into the house. Miss Havisham tried to teach Estella to live without getting emotionally hurt, and Estella is cold-hearted because of it.

Back in London, Wemmick warns Pip not to go home because Compeyson has been watching the apartment. Pips asks Wemmick about the child Jaggers brought to Miss Havisham's and realizes that Molly, Jaggers's maid, is Estella's mother, and that Magwitch is her father.

Magwitch attempts to escape in a boat which is overtaken by Compeyson. Magwitch and Compeyson fight. Compeyson dies, Magwitch is arrested, and the 20,000 pounds sink to the bottom of the Thames. Pip, badly in debt, falls ill and is nursed back to health by Joe and Biddy, an orphan girl who works in her great aunt's shop in the village. Joe has paid Pip's enormous debts and leaves for Kent with Biddy. Pip, who is to sail to India to work as a clerk in Herbert's company, visits Kent to attend Joe's wedding only to find that Joe has married Biddy, Pip's choice for a wife for himself. He realizes at this point that he has lost everything.

Eleven years later Pip is back where he started, in the cemetery where his parents are buried, when he meets Estella who has come to lay flowers on Miss Havisham's grave. Estella asks, "Have you paid all your debts?"

"Yes," Pip answers. "The money ones anyway. I've learned that some accounts can never be paid." Estella's husband, Bentley Drummle, has been killed. Pip says that it has been eleven years, nine months, and five days since they last met. Estella says that they will always be best friends, apart. "Apart?" Pip asks, as the two walk off hand in hand into the mist.

Name _____ Date _____

Great Expectations

True or False, and Why?

Mark the true statements below with a plus (+) and the false statements with a zero (0). Then, on the lines provided, explain *why* the false statements are untrue.

1. _____ Pip wanted to be a gentleman because he thought himself not good enough for Joe.

_____

2. _____ Magwitch funded Pip's life in London because he wished to live in Australia.

_____

3. _____ Miss Havisham realized what she had done to Estella when she heard Pip confessing his love to Estella at Satis House.

_____

4. _____ Pip fell in love with Estella when he was a boy, and loved her all his life.

_____

5. _____ Jaggers was a hard, unfeeling man all his life.

_____

6. _____ Pip laughs at the inscription on Miss Havisham's gravestone because the message was told in the form of a riddle.

_____

7. _____ Miss Havisham's engagement and proposed wedding was a scheme to get revenge for the way she raised Estella.

_____

8. _____ Pip's "expectations" never materialized, while Herbert's did.

_____

9. _____ The lesson Pip learned was that no one escapes the guillotine.

_____

10. _____ Miss Havisham had no pleasant memories of Estella as a child—only regrets.

_____

11. _____ Pip and Biddy were almost exact opposites in their dreams and "expectations."

_____

12. _____ Estella never knew love as a child, and thus was spiteful to her dying day.

_____

Great Expectations

Character Identification

Match the characters listed below with their descriptions by writing their names on the line provided. You may write some characters' names more than once.

Pip	Biddy	Estella	Joe	Herbert
Magwitch	Miss Havisham	Pumblechook	Drummle	Jaggers
Compeyson	Molly	Orlick	Mrs. Joe	Wemmick

1. _____ Believes Miss Havisham is his benefactor

2. _____ Good wife for Joe

3. _____ Miss Havisham's alter ego

4. _____ Is ever the best of friends with Pip

5. _____ Hates being "common"

6. _____ Arrogant brat who marries Pip's dream girl

7. _____ Goes on the "rampage"

8. _____ Murders Mrs. Joe

9. _____ Loving and gentle to the end

10. _____ Estella's mother

11. _____ A shrewd legal mind

12. _____ Miss Havisham's ex-lover

13. _____ Lives in a time warp

14. _____ Funded Pip's "great expectations"

15. _____ Wore one face at work, and another at home

16. _____ Estella's father

17. _____ Called "Handel"

18. _____ Sincere, but unsuccessful friend of Pip

19. _____ Loaned Pip 900 pounds for his best friend

20. _____ A pompous, comical old man

21. _____ Lived in a castle

22. _____ Magwitch's worst enemy

23. _____ Brought Pip up by hand

24. _____ Pip's rival

25. _____ Dotes on his father

Great Expectations

Creative Writing

In the world of *Great Expectations* there were some strong personalities who could qualify for a "Person of the Film" award. Choose one character that in your judgment stands as the person who had the most dramatic impact on events in the story. Write a biographical feature story that reveals this dynamic person to the world. You may use your imagination in re-creating scenes from the person's past, but stick to the facts of the film for the bulk of your story. Offer some insight into the character's mind and make this person come alive for the reader.

The winner of the Person of the Film Award is: _____

_____

_____

_____

_____

Great Expectations

Essay

In a brief essay, tell how the quote below relates to Pip's experience in London—what he learned from the people he met and the things he did.

> *I returned and saw under the sun, that the race is not to the swift, nor the battle to the strong, neither yet bread to the wise, nor yet riches to men of understanding, nor yet favour to men of skill; but time and chance happeneth to them all.*
> —The Book of Ecclesiastes

_____

_____

_____

_____

_____

_____

_____

_____

_____

_____

_____

_____

_____

_____

_____

_____

_____

_____

_____

_____

_____

_____

_____

Great Expectations

Answers

True or False, and Why?

1. 0; Pip thought he had potential to be a fine gentleman; he also believed that life would be more fulfilling if he lived as a proper and wealthy man.

2. 0; Magwitch funded Pip's great expectations because Magwitch wanted to live a gentleman's life through Pip; he wanted to get back at the society that had been so cruel to him.

3. +

4. +

5. 0; Jaggers had a moment of compassion when he saved Estella from a life of hardship and poverty by arranging her adoption by Miss Havisham.

6. 0; Pip laughs because her inscription claims her to be compassionate, when in fact she was heartless, bitter, and cruel most of her life.

7. 0; The scheme which broke Miss Havisham's heart was devised by her brother to punish her for being the sole heir to her wealthy father's estate.

8. +

9. 0; The lesson Pip learned was that no one escapes the trials and tribulations of life, not even the rich who seem to live above and beyond the level of everyone else's sufferings.

10. 0; Miss Havisham had one fond memory of Estella: the night she was brought to Satis House, Estella was smiling in her sleep.

11. +

12. 0; Estella was a tool for revenge at the hands of Miss Havisham, but in the very end she saw how wrong she's been, and how much she could have had if she'd been truly seeking love rather than power over others.

Character Identification

1. Pip	6. Drummle	11. Jaggers	16. Magwitch	21. Wemmick
2. Biddy	7. Mrs. Joe	12. Compeyson	17. Pip	22. Compeyson
3. Estella	8. Orlick	13. Miss Havisham	18. Herbert	23. Mrs. Joe
4. Joe	9. Joe	14. Magwitch	19. Miss Havisham	24. Drummle
5. Pip	10. Molly	15. Wemmick	20. Pumblechook	25. Wemmick

Creative Writing

Sample:

JAGGERS: The brooding, sharp-tongued Jaggers gets the nod as the person of the film *Great Expectations*. His acid tongue and brutally logical mind act as a fence around the actions and reactions of all the characters in the story. Even Miss Havisham is affected; without Jaggers she would not have had access to such a beautiful, doomed child as Estella. Jaggers covered her sin with his legality and set up Estella's mother as his own strange, compliant housekeeper.

Jaggers also poses as the stern opposite to many characters in the film, especially Wemmick and Magwitch. Jaggers serves as an example of the upper-class society of London; he's wealthy, powerful, unfeeling, and legitimate. In his only moment of heart over logic, Jaggers sets up the workings of the entire story by bringing Estella from one set of tragic circumstances into another. This pathetic gesture ensnares the lives of all in the story, from those who inhabit the strange and repressive Satis House to those who slip across the cold, silent surface of the Thames in a feeble attempt to escape London law.

Jaggers is the presence most people fear and respect throughout the story. Some hate him while others just abide in his decisions. Either way, Jaggers affects them one and all.

Essay

Sample:

Like the seeker in the quote from Ecclesiastes, Pip went searching far from home for happiness, truth, and fulfillment in life, and returned empty-handed and wanting in the things he once thought dear. He began his odyssey full of hope in the proprieties of life, in social custom, in money as a means of success and ease, and strongly believed that where he lived and what he had been could not possibly be all there was for him in the world.

He struggled to please a patron who turned out to be a hunted criminal. He fought for social position and lost to a wealthy lout who married the girl of Pip's poor dreams. He bought costly goods in order to appear genteel, but when it all crashed, a loving blacksmith picked up the pieces and gave Pip back his life. And the girl he thought lovely and fine showed herself as a small, manipulative creature who wanted only power, and not love.

Pip learned that nothing could protect him or any person from the trials and agonies of life. All people are subject to the suffering and struggle of human endeavor. Not money, not position, not fame, nor power can make anyone immune from what we all must learn—that life is precious, and the best way to live it is by loving and giving oneself to the service of others. Life without love becomes only a futile chase after substitutes for happiness which make a mockery of us.

BILLY BUDD

Author: Herman Melville
Novel Title: *Billy Budd*
Director: Peter Ustinov

Running Time: 112 minutes
Year: 1962
Format: black and white

Summary

Billy Budd, a young sailor on the merchant ship *Rights of Man*, is impressed onto the British warship *Avenger*. On his first day aboard the *Avenger* Billy witnesses a flogging. "What was the man's crime?" Billy asks. No one knows. The flogging was ordered by Claggart, the ship's enforcer, a wicked, vengeful, complex character with a mysterious past. Billy soon finds out just how cruel Claggart can be. A shipmate, Jenkins, is ordered to attend his post high on the topmast even though he is so sick he can't possibly survive the ordeal. Jenkins plummets to the deck and dies after Billy makes a valiant effort to hang on to Jenkins's hand.

United in their deep hatred of Claggart, the ship's men vow to kill him. But Billy, claiming he doesn't hate Claggart, will have no part of it. One night on deck, Billy talks to Claggart, trying to understand him. When Billy offers to come by at different times to talk, Claggart almost consents, but then bristles, saying, "So you would charm me too?" From that point on Claggart wants Billy destroyed. Later that night Billy wrestles Kincaid, a friend of Jenkins, and takes his knife away—a knife Kincaid was going to use on Claggart who is alone walking the deck. Claggart hears and comes over to break up the fight. When he learns the reason for the fight, he is even more incensed at Billy's goodness.

The next day Claggart embarks on a vicious course of action; he accuses Billy of plotting mutiny. Attempting to defend himself in front of Captain Vere, the ship's commander, Billy stammers and stutters and can't respond. Claggart continues to rail against Billy while the boy builds a fury within himself that can't be contained. He strikes out and knocks Claggart to the floor. Claggart smiles up at Billy, then closes his eyes and dies.

Billy is tried and acquitted on the basis of Captain Vere's testimony, Billy's account of the incident, and the words of Dansker, the elderly sailmaker who tells the court about Claggart's "malice toward a grace he (Claggart) could not have." But the captain intervenes and tells his subordinates that the British Articles of War do not permit acquittal in the case of a seaman striking a superior officer. The verdict has to be death by hanging. The other officers reluctantly agree. Captain Vere pleads with one young officer named Wyatt to find a legal way to release Billy from condemnation, but Wyatt can think of nothing that can be done within the law.

Billy is to be executed the next morning. The men are unsure and nervous about who will be punished. Old Dansker says that it's not a flogging but a hanging, since it's early morning. The men begin to count the missing among their ranks. Claggart is gone! Maybe it's he who will die. "No, he's too smart!" one man says. But Dansker breaks in, "But Claggart is here. He is here."

When Billy steps out onto the deck, the men rail against the captain, howling their disgust and their fear. Billy says nothing. He mounts the deck and stands silently while the noose is slipped over his neck. All are silent, and just before he's hanged, Billy cries, "God Bless Captain Vere!" The captain is visibly shaken and removes his hat, signifying he's done commanding the ship; Seymore must take over. The men are ordered to disperse, but they do not move. Suddenly a French warship opens fire, but still the men do not move. Then Kincaid breaks rank: "C'mon men. Let's make the French pay for turnin' up late!"

The battle is brief. The *Avenger* is beaten. The crew is battered from the barrage and the ship limps off, wounded beyond what anyone, including the French, can know.

Billy Budd

Matching

Match the characters from *Billy Budd* with the quotes listed below. Write the character's name on the line next to each statement he made.

Example: <u>Vere</u> There are some men who can't stand too much perfection.

Billy	Captain Vere	Claggart	Seymore
Dansker	Squeak	Kincaid	

1. _____ Good-bye, old *Rights of Man*!

2. _____ It's wrong to flog a man; it's against his being a man.

3. _____ This sickness gets tedious, Jenkins. Where does it strike you?

4. _____ Kincaid! You're under arrest. Take him below!

5. _____ I suppose a handsome sailor may do many things forbidden to his messmates.

6. _____ He (Jenkins) has got 100 fathoms between him and the troubles of this life.

7. _____ You would charm me too! Get away!

8. _____ No man can take pleasure in cruelty.

9. _____ Every time he laughs at me I know I'm safe.

10. _____ I was sent by Claggart to steal your kit.

11. _____ The living must stand trial for a dead man's crimes.

12. _____ He lied foully to my face and I had to say something.

13. _____ I am only a man, not fit to do the work of God, or the devil.

14. _____ Save him Wyatt, and you save us all!

15. _____ Claggart killed you the moment you killed him.

16. _____ You in your goodness are as inhuman as Claggart was, in his evil.

17. _____ They flog men at noon. Early morning is for hanging.

18. _____ God Bless Captain Vere!

19. _____ C'mon lads! Let's punish the French for turnin' up late!

20. _____ He bore malice toward a grace he could not have.

Billy Budd

Short Answer

1. How did the impending battle with the French affect Billy's trial, and his life?

   _____

   _____

   _____

   _____

2. At the trial, why does Captain Vere's argument, or point of view, win out over the court's decision to acquit Billy?

   _____

   _____

   _____

   _____

3. Why does Dansker take some responsibility for Billy's predicament?

   _____

   _____

   _____

   _____

4. At Billy's trial Dansker says, "…lest his (Claggart's) world be proven false, he planned Billy's death." Describe Claggart's world. How does he view life and human relationships?

   _____

   _____

   _____

   _____

5. What was Claggart's plan to destroy Billy? How could he sure it would work?

   _____

   _____

   _____

   _____

6. What does Dansker mean, at Billy's hanging, when he says, "Claggart is here!"?

   _____

   _____

   _____

   _____

Billy Budd

Symbolism and Metaphor

In great literature, symbols and metaphors play as important a role in communicating the author's vision as dialogue and characterization. The same is true in great films. *Billy Budd* uses the three important metaphors listed below, and two major symbols: the ships *Avenger* and *Rights of Man*.

Explain the metaphors and symbols below in terms of Herman Melville's theme in *Billy Budd*.

1. The war

   _____

   _____

   _____

   _____

2. The sea

   _____

   _____

   _____

   _____

3. The storm

   _____

   _____

   _____

   _____

4. The *Avenger*

   _____

   _____

   _____

   _____

5. The *Rights of Man*

   _____

   _____

   _____

   _____

Billy Budd

Prewriting and Essay

Your assignment is to write an essay titled "Law and Justice: Humanity on Trial." Think about how you might want to approach such a broad topic in reference to the characters, situations, and theme of the film *Billy Budd.* Then use the format below to sketch out your ideas.

- Form a thesis for your essay and write it in the thesis box.
- In the appropriate boxes jot down some definitions, character descriptions, and bits of dialogue that would support your thesis (opinion).
- Then write some transitions that might be helpful in logically organizing your ideas.
- Finally, write a sentence that might make the basis for a sound conclusion to your essay.
- When you have finished jotting down ideas, write your essay on a separate sheet of paper.

Thesis

Definitions

Justice _____

Law _____

Humanity _____

Character Descriptions/Dialogue

Transitions (sentences, phrases, or single words)

Conclusion

Billy Budd

Answers

Matching

1. Billy
2. Billy
3. Claggart
4. Claggart
5. Claggart
6. Dansker
7. Claggart
8. Billy
9. Squeak
10. Squeak
11. Seymore
12. Billy
13. Capt. Vere
14. Capt. Vere
15. Capt. Vere
16. Capt. Vere
17. Dansker
18. Billy
19. Kincaid
20. Dansker

Short Answer

1. With the French close by, Captain Vere believed that Billy's case could not wait to be tried by the admiralty at some later date. The issue had to be dealt with immediately so the *Avenger* could get on with its military mission. This hasty decision cost Billy his life, because possibly once battle conditions were eased, a more compassionate verdict could have been reached.

2. The men are bound by their oath to carry out orders, and Billy's trial and judgment are just two more requirements of the military code to which they have vowed allegiance.

3. Dansker, sensing Claggart's evil nature and the effect of that evil on the entire ship, could have done something about Claggart long ago. But he bowed to fear, and said and did nothing.

4. Life is like the dark depths of the sea—fearsome, and violent. Everyone is out to survive, which means everyone will do whatever is necessary to secure a place for himself, even if it means killing and destroying one's fellow creatures.

5. Claggart knew Billy's weakness. He knew Billy would not be able to defend himself with words, and that Billy's sense of justice would force him to lash out when confronted by such vile injustice. By striking his superior officer, Billy would be condemned to death.

6. Claggart's spirit prevailed in the destruction of Billy. It wasn't Claggart the man but Claggart the beast, the innocence-killing beast, that wanted Billy destroyed. And that spirit was among the men like a bad wind on the day of Billy's hanging.

Symbolism and Metaphor

1. The war which Captain Vere says has been going on long before his time is the war between good and evil within men's souls. The response to that war has been to set up a system of laws that protects innocence and punishes evil. The battle raging on the sea is an extension of the battle on the deck of the *Avenger* between justice and the letter of the law.

2. The sea is populated with millions of different creatures who must live in the same ecosystem, who must kill and devour lesser creatures in order to survive—"A place of gliding monsters, murderers all," says Claggart.

3. The storm referred to by Dansker on the night before Billy's trial is the metaphor for the storm brewing within Claggart's wicked soul. His hatred of innocence (expressed in the life of Billy Budd) has put a pressure on the lives of all aboard. The cataclysm is about to descend upon Billy, and upon the entire crew of the *Avenger*.

4. The *Avenger* is a ship whose name symbolizes man's approach to wrongdoing. Claggart, on the one hand, is avenging the "wrongs" done to him by the world (in accusing Billy), and Captain Vere is trying to avenge the wrong done to Billy by holding a trial. But the *Avenger* becomes a ship of fools and destroys itself by not applying justice to the workings of the law. To avenge a wrong by using the law, one runs the risk of destroying the principle around which law was initially conceived: justice for all.

5. The *Rights of Man* is a ship in sharp contrast to the *Avenger*. The *Rights of Man* symbolizes the simple justice afforded those who live by the spirit of the law, by the rights which law was meant to protect, rather than by the workings and dealings of the law itself. The ship *Rights of Man* sails away, independent and whole and solid, while the *Avenger* lies smoking and beaten just off the rocks of an unnamed island at film's end.

Prewriting and Essay

Answers will vary.

A SEPARATE PEACE

Author: John Knowles
Novel Title: *A Separate Peace*
Director: Larry Pearce

Running Time: 104 minutes
Year: 1972
Format: color

Summary

This is a film about war, not between countries or principalities, but within the human heart. Can people love and hate in the same moment? What if we listen to our hate, even for an instant? Will we destroy somebody? Will we destroy ourselves?

In the opening scene a middle-aged man walks across the campus of a New England prep school. Standing beneath a tall, sparsely limbed tree, he remembers what happened there and what he caused to happen and says, "I guess nothing endures—not a tree, not love, not even a death by violence."

Then, in a flashback, the scene explodes with the brassy music of a 1940's dance band and a golden-haired, clear-eyed boy racing across a green carrying a lacrosse stick. Several boys throw open their dorm windows and yell, "Hey, Finny! Wait for me!"

Finny, the bold, brassy, loving hero of the story is liked by everyone, even the headmaster, who catches Finny at a social tea wearing a school tie for a belt and doesn't expel him—a response from authority toward a boy whose lust for life is only exceeded by his ability to love.

Finny's roommate and best friend is Gene, the school's valedictorian. Gene is fair-haired, thin, and admired for his brains. He is brave when pushed to be so, committed to keeping his grades up, and capable of enough friendliness to make him acceptable to most of his classmates. But he has a dark side, a latent violence that even he does not know is in him until a fateful day in the summer when Finny asks him to once again climb the high limb of the tree on the river bank and perform a "double jump." Others had been teased to do it in earlier episodes, but only Gene would climb so high and leap to the water below. Leper, the school's resident "deep thinker," was called a coward by the hardline student Brinker. Finny said it was all right; Leper didn't have to jump. "We need guys like you around, Leper," Finny said, and thus exhibited his greatest quality—a loving heart.

After a day at the beach where Finny tells Gene, "The proper person to come to the beach with is your best pal, which is what you are," the two go to the tree and climb to the high limb. Gene jounces the limb and Finny falls, shattering his leg. Gene looks down at his fallen friend, then makes a cool, collected dive into the river.

Finny is taken home to recuperate, and Gene visits him and confesses. Finny refuses to believe his friend could do such a thing, but says in anger, "Go away. I'm tired, and you make me sick." Finny calls Gene later talking as if they'd had a fight. But the truth lies deeper than that.

Brinker, a zealous, hard-edged pragmatist sets up a trial to set the record straight. All the boys of their class are present in black robes and the questions begin. Finny lies for Gene and says Gene was at the bottom of the tree and not even on the limb. But then Brinker says that he has an eyewitness: Leper. Leper was supposed to jump that day to prove his bravery, and upon nearing the tree saw the boys on the limb. He testifies and Finny hobbles out of the room in a fury and falls down the stairs. He has broken his other leg cleanly and is put in the infirmary.

Gene visits Finny, who confronts him with what he did. Gene says, "It was ignorance inside me, something crazy, something blind." Finny replies, "I believe you."

When Finny's bone is set, a bit of marrow gets into his bloodstream and kills him. Gene says, "I couldn't get over the feeling that it was my own funeral. And you don't cry in that case."

A Separate Peace

Multiple Choice

Write the letter of the correct answer on the line next to each item.

1. _____ *A Separate Peace* takes place at a: (a) military academy (b) reform school (c) private preparatory high school (d) military camp

2. _____ The main characters in the movie are: (a) Finny (b) Bill (c) Quackenbush (d) Professor Ludbury (e) Gene (f) Fence (g) Albert (h) a and b (i) a and c (j) a and d (k) a and e (l) a and f (m) a, b, and f (n) a, b, and e (o) a, b, and g

3. _____ Leper shows that he is the most sensitive and perceptive of the group because he: (a) recognizes Gene's savage nature (b) recognizes Finny's inherently good nature (c) recognizes the corruption within himself (d) a and b (e) a and c (f) a, b, and c

4. _____ People generally follow along with Finny because: (a) his enthusiasm is contagious (b) they admire Finny because he's a gifted athlete (c) he has no harmful feelings toward people (d) he keeps things interesting (e) a and b (f) a and c (g) a, b, and c (h) a, b, c, and d

5. _____ After Finny falls from the tree, Gene dives gracefully and calmly into the river because: (a) he feels guilty (b) he is afraid that Finny is dead (c) he wants to dive rather than jump, in honor of his dead friend (d) he feels victorious (e) a and b (f) a, b, c, and d

6. _____ When Gene confesses to Finny, Finny rejects his confession because: (a) Finny distrusts Gene's motives (b) he doesn't want to believe Gene would do such a thing (c) he is afraid of what Gene will do next (d) he can't bear to betray his friend

7. _____ Finny's greatest talent was his ability to: (a) break long-held school records with ease (b) keep his accomplishments to himself (c) forgive (d) make others happy (e) a and c

8. _____ The irony of the trial that Brinker organizes is that: (a) Brinker actually hates Gene (b) the truth is told by the most distorted mind on campus (c) Finny didn't believe that Gene intentionally rocked the tree limb (d) Gene was exposed as a liar

9. _____ Gene tells Finny that he (Finny) would "really mess up a war." This is an ironic statement because: (a) by messing it up, Finny would bring people together and probably save a lot of lives (b) Gene is already messed up (c) Finny can't even join the service, he's too young.

10. _____ By the end of the movie, Gene learns that: (a) nothing lasts forever (b) all relationships are built on a mixture of love and hate (c) he is capable of murder (d) life is fragile (e) a and b (f) a, b, and c (g) a, b, c, and d (h) none of the above

11. _____ Near the end of the film the doctor says that war and the operating room share a common characteristic: (a) the risk of death (b) the certainty of loneliness (c) high cost in dollars and cents (d) the need for a specific strategy (e) a and c

12. _____ Gene comes to a separate peace because: (a) he knew it would turn out this way (b) he kept apart from everyone (c) he was in a separate war with himself (d) he was the only one who could have saved Finny (e) he alone believed Leper

Name _____ Date _____

A Separate Peace

Character Identification

Below are statements made by the four characters **Brinker, Gene, Finny**, and **Leper**. Write the first letter of the character's name on the line next to the statements he made.

1. _____ I don't believe books, and I don't believe teachers, but I do believe you.
2. _____ You'll have your day in court!
3. _____ Something just seized you; it wasn't anything personal.
4. _____ You always were a savage underneath.
5. _____ What do you like least about my character?
6. _____ Finny, I tried to tell you the first time.
7. _____ They were going to give me a section 8; they said I was nuts.
8. _____ I couldn't get over the feeling that it was my own funeral.
9. _____ If you don't stop pitying him he'll start pitying himself.
10. _____ Gifted people don't have to strain or do anything unpleasant.
11. _____ You'd make a terrible mess out of the war.
12. _____ Did you come here to abuse me?
13. _____ The sun's rays were shooting past them like golden machine-gun fire.
14. _____ If the war can drive somebody nuts, it's real.
15. _____ Go away. I'm tired and you make me sick.
16. _____ You think I'm a fool, but I'm not a fool anymore!
17. _____ C'mon, let's do a double jump.
18. _____ I have no interest in the war effort.
19. _____ It was ignorance inside me, something crazy, something blind.
20. _____ The two of them looked as black as death.

Name _____   Date _____

A Separate Peace

Short Essay

Put yourself in Finny's place, out on the limb of the "diving tree." Who would you want to have standing on the limb with you? What is it about this person that makes you trust him or her? How does he or she think? What does he or she want out of life?

When the chips are down, when it really matters, can you count on this person? How do you know?

Write a short essay defending your choice of a trusted friend. Make up a name if you don't want to use the person's real name.

I would trust _____

      because: _____

_____

_____

_____

_____

_____

_____

_____

_____

_____

_____

_____

_____

_____

_____

_____

_____

_____

_____

_____

_____

_____

_____

_____

_____

A Separate Peace

Literary Terms

Below is a list of literary terms that can apply to an art form whether it be a play, a painting, a novel, or a film. Think of examples of the terms as they appeared in the movie *A Separate Peace*. Then write them on the lines provided in each item below.

TERMS: **conflict, climax, metaphor, imagery, symbolism, flashback**

1. Describe the greatest moment of **conflict** in Finny's life. What caused the conflict?

   _____

   _____

   _____

2. When was the true **climax** of the story? When Finny fell from the limb? When Leper returned?

   _____

   _____

   _____

3. How does World War II act as a **metaphor** in the story? A metaphor for what?

   _____

   _____

   _____

4. What example of **imagery** touched you the most in this film? Why?

   _____

   _____

   _____

5. How is the tree an example of **symbolism**? What does it represent?

   _____

   _____

   _____

6. Why do you think the author, John Knowles, used the **flashback** technique to tell this story?

   _____

   _____

   _____

A Separate Peace

Answers

Multiple Choice

1. c	5. d	9. a
2. k	6. b	10. g
3. f	7. c	11. a
4. h	8. b	12. c

Character Identification

1. F	6. G	11. G	16. L
2. B	7. L	12. L	17. F
3. F	8. G	13. L	18. L
4. L	9. B	14. F	19. G
5. F	10. F	15. F	20. L

Literary Terms

1. The greatest moment of conflict for Finny was at the trial when he realized that Gene had really intended to hurt him, or even kill him. Finny, in his openheartedness, never thought such evil toward him was possible, especially from his best friend.

2. The climax of the story was when Leper told what he saw, and Gene and Finny had to face the truth: Gene tried to kill Finny because of an envious moment during a childish act of daring.

3. The metaphor of war is carried to the lawns of Devon through the character of Gene who has declared war against everyone around him. He battles for the best standing among his peers, is ambitious, and "savage underneath," as Leper said. The irony, tragedy, and loss of innocent life happened at Devon as it does in all wars.

4. The image of the stark, dark-skinned tree hanging its leafless limbs out over the water appears as a cross of crucifixion for the innocent, free-spirited Finny. It is a living tombstone for Finny, and is a monument to Gene's lost ignorance about his own capacity for evil.

5. The tree is a symbol of death. It has no leaves as we see it from the present, through Gene's eyes. It is a cross of crucifixion for Finny, and a hanging tree for Gene. It is a symbol of life in the midst of death.

6. By having Gene relive the scene of the tragedy, we get a sense of the time lapse that occurred and we get a mature view of how the outcome of such violence continues long after the event.

Short Essay

Answers will vary.

A PASSAGE TO INDIA

Author: E.M. Forster
Novel Title: *A Passage to India*
Director: David Lean

Running Time: 163 minutes
Year: 1984
Format: color

Summary

A young Englishwoman, Adela Quested, books passage to India with an elderly woman, Mrs. Moore, who is the mother of Adela's intended husband, Ronny Heaslop (Ronny is the son of Mrs. Moore's first husband). Both women are tense with excitement at the thought of visiting exotic India. On arrival they meet the Turtons, an aristocratic English couple who practice a vicious racism toward the Indian people. The women are disgusted with this "English outlook."

One night an Indian named Dr. Aziz is called to the office of a high official. Aziz goes to the office and, finding no one there, walks to a mosque to meditate. An unfamiliar Englishwoman, Mrs. Moore, enters. They talk and find that they have much in common: They have both lost their spouse and each has two children. Aziz is taken with the kindness of Mrs. Moore, who is unlike any English person he has met.

At a social gathering held to fulfill Mrs. Moore's request to meet some of the native people of India, Adela meets Mr. Fielding, president of the Government College in Chandrapore. He arranges a meeting between the women and a Professor Godbole; Aziz will be there too. At the gathering, Aziz proposes a trip to the Marabar Caves, many hours by train from Chandrapore. Professor Godbole is unsettled by the plan, but doesn't say why. Mrs. Moore is upset by Godbole's hesitancy to explain the caves.

The next day Adela goes to an abandoned temple where she is bothered by a sense of mystery and terror. Suddenly a pack of wild monkeys run at her from their place among the statues, and she flees in terror. That night Adela dreams of the statues and is troubled by the wind.

Fielding misses the train to the caves the next morning, but promises to catch up by automobile.

At the caves, Mrs. Moore is bothered by claustrophobia and by a lingering dread. The caves seem to hold some evil, some threat that can't be described. At Mrs. Moore's suggestion, Aziz and Adela go on alone to the upper caves. While there, Aziz leaves to smoke a cigarette. Adela steps into a cave by herself. She begins to tremble and succumb to the power of the echo and the darkness. When Aziz comes to the cave calling for her, she blows out her match to hide from him. In the next scene she runs down the mountain, gets caught in a thorn bush, and tears herself horribly before escaping into the car that has just dropped off Mr. Fielding.

Back in Chandrapore, Adela claims that Aziz tried to rape her. A trial is held. Tensions are high. Mrs. Moore, Aziz's key witness, leaves for England and dies of heart failure on the ship; she is buried at sea. The crowd roars for Mrs. Moore, unaware that she is dead. Meanwhile Adela takes the stand and recants, admitting that Aziz had done nothing and that she had been wrong in accusing him. The trial is aborted. The English consider her insane and hate her for recalling her word, which they feel should be respected and feared by the Indian people. Fielding takes her home where she finds out about Mrs. Moore's death. Godbole arrives while the city is preparing a celebration in honor of Aziz. He says good-bye to Fielding and leaves for his new post as minister of education.

Aziz is furious because of the shame brought on him by "an English girl who got too much sun!" Fielding pleads her case (Aziz's lawyer wants 20,000 rupees in damages) and Aziz says, "In the end you English always stick together."

Fielding goes back to England and marries Mrs. Moore's daughter, Stella. He writes to Aziz, who is holding a grudge and tears up the missives. Finally, Godbole intercedes and arranges a meeting between Fielding and Aziz at which Aziz meets Stella Moore. When Aziz sees Mrs. Moore's kindness showing forth through her daughter, he is deeply touched and writes Adela a letter asking forgiveness for his inability to recognize her courage in aborting the trial. The last scene shows Adela reading the letter, then walking off with a new look of resolve in her face.

A Passage to India

Multiple Choice

Mark the true statements below with a plus sign (+) and mark the false statements with a zero (0).

1. _____ Adela Quested books passage to India with the hope of encountering adventure.

2. _____ Mrs. Moore says she loves mysteries, but hates "muddles" where there is no ending.

3. _____ Early in the film Dr. Aziz's friend said that the reason the Indians talked so much about the British was because the Indians admired them.

4. _____ Dr. Aziz is in many ways childish and impulsive.

5. _____ Dr. Aziz asks the women to the Marabar Caves to avoid having to invite them to his home.

6. _____ To many Englishmen, Mr. Fielding is considered a comrade and true patriot.

7. _____ Adela loves Ronny Heaslop, but hates his racism towards the Indians.

8. _____ The Marabar Caves have a reputation for exerting mysterious forces upon people who are sensitive to such powers.

9. _____ Professor Godbole was pleased that he suggested the women visit the Marabar Caves when he met Mrs. Moore in the mosque on her first night in India.

10. _____ Fielding has earned the respect of the Indian people because he is not a snob.

11. _____ Dr. Aziz's plan worked perfectly; Mrs. Moore could not endure the caves, which left him totally alone with Adela Quested.

12. _____ Adela, at one point, seemed to be emotionally drawn toward Dr. Aziz during their trip to the upper caves.

13. _____ In the cave Adela blew out her match to hide herself from Dr. Aziz, because she imagined he was coming to molest her.

14. _____ Adela was clearly insane at the time of the trial.

15. _____ Mr. Fielding was promoted to Minister of Education for his support of Dr. Aziz.

16. _____ Aziz was angry with Fielding because he sided with Miss Quested.

17. _____ Miss Quested finally wrote a letter of apology to Dr. Aziz, which helped heal their broken friendship.

18. _____ Professor Godbole intervened to bring Aziz and Fielding together again.

19. _____ Aziz learned to appreciate Miss Quested's courage in calling off the trial.

20. _____ The film presents a journey within a journey as Adela Quested traveled to India, then to the caves, then to the inner reaches of her own soul as she grew into maturity.

A Passage to India

Matching

Match the speakers to their lines of dialogue by writing the letter of the speaker next to the line that he or she spoke during the film.

Example: __f__ "I'm sure the professor and Aziz would agree that India is a "'muddle.'"

a. Dr. Aziz	e. Professor Godbole
b. Adela Quested	f. Mr. Fielding
c. Mr. Turton	g. Ronny Heaslop
d. Mrs. Moore	h. McBryde the prosecutor

1. _____ "In the end you English always stick together!"

2. _____ "Life is a wheel with many spokes."

3. _____ "Did you see Aziz? Dressed to the hilt, and no collar button!"

4. _____ "Mrs. Moore is an 'old soul.'"

5. _____ "We can hold a 'bridge party' if you like."

6. _____ "I'm not a missionary. I'm just a member of the civil service."

7. _____ "The whole purpose of this entertainment is an exercise in power and the subtle pleasures of superiority!"

8. _____ "You married my enemy. Stole my money!"

9. _____ "I had a small adventure. And saw the moon in the Ganges!"

10. _____ "We are in the same box, Mrs. Moore."

11. _____ "What a terrible river; what a wonderful river!"

12. _____ "I'm a doctor. Snakes don't dare bite me."

13. _____ "Did you have more than one wife, Dr. Aziz?"

14. _____ "Miss Quested. Tell the court exactly what happened."

15. _____ "I realized then that I didn't love Ronny."

16. _____ "Can you not let bygones be bygones and show them around?"

17. _____ "Aziz is an innocent!"

18. _____ "Of course he's innocent. Something else must have happened."

19. _____ "It took me all these years to appreciate your courage, Miss Quested."

20. _____ "If Dr. Aziz is convicted, I'll resign my position at the college!"

A Passage to India

Symbolism

A great writer uses many techniques to communicate meaning. In *A Passage to India*, E.M. Forster uses the names of his characters to suggest personality traits. Adela Quested is unequivocally "addled"; she has mixed feelings about her betrothed, Ronny Heaslop, and has a vague longing for adventure and excitement. Her judgment is flawed by her lack of maturity and understanding and she, in the end, makes the wild claim against Dr. Aziz that gives the story its highest tension.

Forster's technique is repeated with the other characters listed below. In the space provided, explain what the name brings to mind.

Adela Quested—What kind of "quest" is she on?

_____

_____

_____

_____

_____

Mr. Turton—What creature does he resemble in his stance and attitude?

_____

_____

_____

_____

_____

Ronny Heaslop—How is he "high"? How is he "sloppy" in his treatment of people?

_____

_____

_____

_____

_____

Mrs. Moore—How is she "more" of a person than the average Englishwoman in India?

_____

_____

_____

_____

_____

A Passage to India

Essay

E.M. Forster seems to be saying that we all make a passage to our own "India" at some point in our lives. As Mrs. Moore said in the film, "India forces one to come to terms with oneself."

On the lines below, tell about a time in your life when you found out something about yourself that may not have been pleasant to learn. Did you go through an experience, move to a place, or visit someone, where you did something unusual, seemingly out of character, which you had to admit to and for which you had to take responsibility? If you cannot recall any such experience, talk to friends (peers or adults), and listen to their story of a journey they took "into themselves," where they discovered that they were only human after all.

_____

_____

_____

_____

_____

_____

_____

_____

_____

_____

_____

_____

_____

_____

_____

_____

_____

_____

_____

_____

_____

_____

_____

_____

A Passage to India

Answers

True or False

1. +	6. 0	11. 0	16. +
2. +	7. 0	12. +	17. 0
3. +	8. +	13. +	18. +
4. +	9. 0	14. 0	19. +
5. +	10. +	15. 0	20. +

Matching

1. a	6. g	11. d	16. e
2. e	7. d	12. a	17. f
3. g	8. a	13. b	18. d
4. e	9. d	14. h	19. a
5. c	10. a	15. b	20. f

Symbolism

Possible answers:

Adela Quested—Miss *Quest*ed is on an adventure. She is searching for something strange, exotic, and wonderful. It is not just a social call. She is after something, and her quest takes her to the depths of her own fears and failings.

Mr. Turton—He is turtlelike in his appearance and manner. His old, wrinkled, expressionless face and heavy-eyed look give the impression that he is not easily moved off course. He hides beneath a shell of bigotry and racism and won't come out to see the light (truth) of day.

Ronny Heaslop—Mr. Heaslop has moved *up* the ladder of power in the English aristocracy where he has a high position in government. His sloppiness is expressed in the cold, careless way in which he views and treats the natives of the country.

Mrs. Moore—Mrs. Moore has *more* to offer in the way of kindness and true understanding than any other Englishwoman in Chandrapore. She has compassion and a deep sense of life's eternal truths. She is more human, more holy than any of those around her.

Essay

Essays will vary.

A MAN FOR ALL SEASONS

Author: Robert Bolt
Play Title: *A Man for All Seasons*
Director: Fred Zinneman

Running Time: 134 minutes
Year: 1966
Format: color

Summary

Sir Thomas More, a vibrant, conscientious, brilliant judge in King Henry VIII's court, is summoned by Cardinal Wolsey, chancellor of England, to Hampton Court to discuss why Thomas opposed him in the council earlier that day. "Because I thought you were wrong," Thomas says, and with that the central conflict of the story unfolds.

The king of England wants to divorce his wife Catherine, who has given him no heir, and marry Anne Boleyn. But he can't divorce without the consent of the pope, who recently gave a dispensation to King Henry to marry Catherine, the widow of the king's brother, in the first place. The king has charged his administrators with the job of "convincing" the pope to grant the needed dispensation, but all of these men and their efforts have failed.

The man, above all others, who might have a chance with the pope is Sir Thomas More, a devout Catholic with an integrity not seen since Plato, according to his friend, Howard, the duke of Norfolk. But Thomas will have none of the king's politics insofar as they contradict the Church.

Wolsey dies and Henry VIII chooses Sir Thomas to become his next lord chancellor, a powerful position, both politically and religiously. Thomas still refuses, very discreetly, to sanction the king's divorce. The king is displeased, but promises to keep Thomas "out of it."

Shortly thereafter, King Henry establishes his own church, separate from the Roman Catholic Church, called the Church of England, of which he, Henry, is the supreme head. Thomas resigns because he says this is "war against the church." Henry immediately appoints a cunning, vicious politician named Cromwell to "minimize the inconveniences" caused by Henry's decision to form the church, declare his own marriage null and void, and marry Anne Boleyn.

Pressure mounts as Sir Thomas is questioned about alleged bribes when he was in office, about communicating with a deceased prophetess, the Holy Maid of Kent, and about instigating and writing a book called *In Defense of the Seven Sacraments* and publishing it under the king's name. None of these accusations last more than a minute under Sir Thomas's astute rebuttals, and Thomas is excused "for the present." Thomas ends his friendship with the duke of Norfolk, staging a fight at the waterfront in order to clear his friend of all suspicion. He also refuses to make any statement to his wife, Alice, or daughter, Meg, about the king's divorce. Thomas believes that remaining silent will ensure his life and the lives of his loved ones.

He is wrong. The king passes an oath through Parliament that all loyal subjects must sign. Thomas refuses because the oath sanctions and blesses the king's divorce. Chancellor Cromwell imprisons Sir Thomas in the Tower of London and proceeds to interrogate him. A treacherous assistant (former acquaintance of Sir Thomas) named Richard Rich aids Cromwell in his investigation, but to no avail. Thomas remains silent, which under English law keeps him from indictment.

The climax is the court scene where Thomas is now accused of high treason, and in a powerful argument Sir Thomas More presents a brilliant lesson in English common law to a packed courtroom. Silence (refusal to sign the oath) according to English law is an act of consent, not denial. So if members of the court wish to construe anything from Thomas's silence, then they construe that. But he is betrayed by false testimony from the lips of Richard Rich and is condemned to death. Thomas says, "I do none harm, I say none harm, I think none harm, and if this is not enough to keep a man alive, then in good faith, I long not to live." He is executed soon after.

A Man for All Seasons

True or False and Short Answer

Mark the true statements below with a plus sign (+) and the false statements with a zero (0).

1. _____ Cardinal Wolsey laughed when Sir Thomas More suggested that the country should be governed by prayer.

2. _____ Cardinal Wolsey's title was chancellor of England.

3. _____ Before he died, Wolsey succeeded in getting the Church to grant a dispensation so the king could divorce his wife and marry Anne Boleyn.

4. _____ The king promised to keep Thomas out of the conflict with the church over the subject of the divorce.

5. _____ At the trial, Richard Rich turned out to be Sir Thomas's one true ally.

6. _____ Thomas More did not care whom the king married as long as the woman was not a heretic.

7. _____ The king wanted a divorce because his wife was his brother's widow, and their marriage was scripturally unsound according to Leviticus, chapter 18, verse 16.

8. _____ According to Sir Thomas More, God's authority is supreme over all the institutions and laws of man.

9. _____ According to historical account, Richard Rich was beheaded for high treason five years after the king's death.

10. _____ The evidence that ended Sir Thomas's chance for release was the testimony that he occasionally took bribes in his role as judge.

Fill in the blanks below with the correct information.

The film opens with Sir Thomas More traveling in the middle of the night to meet with

(11.) _____. He would not support the king's divorce because the

pope had just given a (12.) _____ for the king to marry Catherine,

his brother's widow, a few years before. For refusing to help, Thomas was later forced to resign

his commission as (13.) _____ and live as a common man. When Sir

Thomas let his servants go he said, "I am no longer a (14.) _____

man, so I do not need a great household." This was ironic of course because

(15.) _____ was the only court official or officer of the church to stand up

to the king and refuse to sign the (16.) _____. Thomas was then

interrogated by Master Secretary (17.) _____. But Thomas knew the

law and believed that as long as he maintained (18.) _____ he could

not be rightfully accused of anything, especially treason. He was surprised, then, on the day of

the trial to actually learn that he was going to be (19.) _____. It was

the testimony of (20.) _____ _____ that doomed him, yet

Thomas felt only grief at the man having (21.) _____ himself before

the court and before God.

Name _____   Date _____

A Man for All Seasons

Vocabulary

Below is a list of words used in the movie *A Man for All Seasons*. Write the word that best completes each sentence on the line provided. Look up words you are unsure of in your dictionary.

obscure	discreet	construe
blithe	clamor	temporal
rebuke	iniquitous	immunity
beseech	conscience	indictment
mutable	loathe	repugnant

1. Sir Thomas More believed that one should always follow one's _____.

2. "The court must _____ what I say according to the law," said Sir Thomas.

3. The _____ against Sir Thomas was based on no real evidence.

4. When the guards came to wake Sir Thomas for interrogation, Thomas growled, "This is _____."

5. God's heavenly laws take precedence over any _____ authority.

6. God's laws are not _____; they are always the same.

7. Sir Thomas was wary and thus very _____ when talking with the king about the divorce.

8. "I would be _____ to think that I would deny my conscience," Thomas said.

9. The loud _____ raised by the king over Thomas's refusal to bless the marriage to Anne Boleyn was childish and unnecessary.

10. Meg came to Thomas's cell to _____ him to sign the king's oath.

11. Sir Thomas _____ (d) Richard Rich for not being honest and straightforward.

12. Sir Thomas said that the Church should not come under attack by the king because it was promised _____ in the Magna Carta and in the king's own coronation oath.

13. The thought of giving in and signing the king's oath was _____ to Sir Thomas.

14. Thomas kept his statements about the king's divorce purposely unclear and _____ in order to protect his loved ones from investigation; what they didn't know could save them.

15. "God will not refuse one who is so _____ to go to him," Thomas said.

A Man for All Seasons

Interview

Sir Thomas says to Richard Rich early in the film, "Why not be a teacher? You'd be a fine teacher, perhaps a great one."

"Who would know it?" Richard replies.

"You—your pupils—your friends—and God; not a bad public, that. And oh, you'd have a quiet life."

Interview the person you feel qualifies as the best teacher in your school. Ask that teacher if Thomas More is right. Start with easy questions about his or her background, experience, education, hobbies, and so forth, and then get to the serious issues.

- What do you like most about teaching? What do you dislike?
- What would you like to see changed in today's educational system?
- What is education's role in shaping the future?
- What do you feel personally responsible for in teaching your students?
- Where do you feel your responsibility ends when it comes to students?
- What do you feel parents could do to help their children succeed in school?
- What is your personal definition of success?
- Have you ever felt that you completely failed at something? What was it? What happened as a result of that failure?
- Whom do you admire most in education today? Fifty years ago? Five hundred years ago?
- What do you fear will happen to schools in the future?
- What will students need to know 10 years from now? 20 years from now?
- What were your elementary, middle school, and high school days like?
- What part of school did you, as a child, dislike the most? Like the most?
- What are your personal goals as a teacher?
- What kinds of classes are most important to today's students?
- If you couldn't teach, what career would you prefer?
- What is your biggest fear in life?
- Define "respect" and tell what part it plays in your classroom.
- What is your opinion of today's generation of teenagers?
- If you could change one thing in your teaching, what would it be?
- If you could do it all over again, would you be a teacher? Why or why not?

After asking as many of these questions as you and the teacher are comfortable with, write up the interview (this is called "transcribing your notes"), show the final story to your teacher for approval, and if possible, have it published in the school newspaper.

A Man for All Seasons

Essay

Write an essay about one of the topics below. If you choose a quotation, explain what it means and give your opinion about it, using the questions as a guide. Conclude your essay in a separate paragraph that includes a strong statement confirming your beliefs as stated earlier in your thesis.

1. "When statesmen forsake their conscience for their sense of duty, they lead their country into chaos."—Sir Thomas More. Do you agree or disagree? What is "conscience"? How do you define "duty"? What examples can you give of national "chaos"?

2. "A man [woman] should go where he [she] is not tempted."—Sir Thomas More. What does Thomas mean by "go"? How are people tempted? Is all temptation bad? What does Thomas mean by "temptation"? Is he right or wrong? Defend your opinion.

3. "If I had served God half as well as I have served my king, God would not have left me here to die in this place."—Cardinal Wolsey. What does Wolsey mean by "serving"? What would Wolsey's life have been like had he done what he said he should have? In your opinion, how would different behavior on Wolsey's part have changed the events in the film?

4. "I'd give the devil benefit of the law for my own safety's sake!"—Sir Thomas More. What does Thomas mean? Why is law so important in a society? Do we protect ourselves when we protect others' rights? Who should come under the protection of the law? In your opinion, what is the value of laws in human societies?

5. "The lord chancellor [Sir Thomas] is an innocent man."—Master Cromwell. Define "innocence." Was Thomas innocent? In what ways was he or was he not innocent? Is innocence a worthwhile virtue? Is there a better way to "be"? In your opinion can an "innocent" person exist in today's society.

6. "When a man [or woman] takes an oath, he is holding his life in his hands like water."—Sir Thomas More. What does this simile means? What is an "oath"? In what way is an oath connected to our character, to who we are? What happens if we break an oath? Can you say one thing and believe another? In your opinion, are oaths dangerous things to be avoided, or are they the cornerstone of law and order in a chaotic world? Defend your opinion.

7. Explain the meaning of the title of the film *A Man for All Seasons*. To what "seasons" does the title refer? And how is Sir Thomas the man for them?

8. Define "conscience" and explain its value (or lack of value) to human life in general and to your life in particular.

9. Define "corruption" and explain its effect on the quality of human life as you know it.

10. Define "cowardice" and tell how it applies first to the theme of *A Man for All Seasons* and then to your own experience. Have you ever acted cowardly? How do you know it was cowardly behavior? What were the effects of your cowardice, or of someone else's whom you trusted? What does *A Man for All Seasons* tell us about cowardice?

A Man for All Seasons

Answers

True or False and Short Answer

1. +	6. 0	11. Cardinal Wolsey	16. oath	21. perjured
2. +	7. 0	12. dispensation	17. Cromwell	
3. 0	8. +	13. chancellor	18. silence	
4. +	9. 0	14. great	19. executed	
5. 0	10. 0	15. Thomas	20. Richard Rich	

Vocabulary

1. conscience	6. mutable	11. rebuke
2. construe	7. discreet	12. immunity
3. indictment	8. loathe	13. repugnant
4. iniquitous	9. clamor	14. obscure
5. temporal	10. beseech	15. blithe

Interview

Responses will vary.

Essay

Essays will vary.

OF MICE AND MEN

Author: John Steinbeck
Novel Title: *Of Mice and Men*
Director: Reza Badiyi

Running Time: 125 minutes
Year: 1981
Format: color

Summary

George Milton and Lennie Small share a dream: a place of their own. But as itinerant farmhands they can never raise enough money. Their main problem is Lennie, a baby in a giant's body. He loves to touch soft things and most recently grabbed onto a little girl's dress and wouldn't let go. A mob is after them as the film opens, and they have stopped to visit Lennie's Aunt Clara for some food and rest. Frustrated, George tries to dump Lennie at Clara's by hitching a ride on a flatbed truck, but in the end he goes back for his friend. The mob finds them and George and Lennie run for their lives. They scramble up a steep river bank, after being chased across a field, and escape.

They arrive at a ranch ready to earn a stake to buy their dream place. There they meet Candy, the old bunkhouse swamper (handyman); Slim, the ranch foreman; Carlson, a sturdy ranch hand; and Curley, the ranch owner's small, mean, son who is obsessed with proving his manhood.

Curley is immediately threatened by Lennie, a giant in any crowd, and proceeds to bully him whenever he can. Candy says, "He hates big guys," and George tells Lennie to stay away from Curley, but to "Give it to him" if he ever starts anything. "Give him what, George?" Lennie asks.

May, Curley's lonely wife, takes every opportunity to visit with the ranch hands. The men avoid her, which makes May crave their companionship even more. One day Curley charges into the bunkhouse looking for his wife, then charges out again suspecting Slim is with her. The bunkhouse empties as the men follow Curley to see the fight. When all is quiet, George further instructs Lennie to avoid Curley and Lennie says, "Tell it, George, 'bout the way it's gonna be."

George tells Lennie that no one has what they've got, each other; that they'll get a place with a few acres, and they'll have rabbits for Lennie to tend. George says he knows of just such a place that's for sale for $600, and Candy, who is curled up on a nearby bunk mourning the death of his old dog, Mack, speaks up, "I've got $300. And I'll throw in with you." George agrees and the three rejoice in their dream come true. Curley returns with Slim and apologizes about May. Hearing Lennie chuckling about the rabbits, Curley turns on him and pummels him with his fists. To stop the blows, Lennie crushes Curley's hand.

Once May finds out that Lennie was the real cause of Curley's "accident," she taunts Curley and Curley throws her out. The next day she goes to the barn to get a puppy. There she finds Lennie who has just killed one of the pups by slapping it after it nipped him. Lennie tells her of his love of soft things, and she lets him touch her hair. When May starts to pull away, Lennie's grip tightens. She screams. Trying to quiet her, Lennie breaks her neck. Knowing that he's "done a bad thing," he runs out, and hides by the river where he and George camped earlier.

After Candy and George find May's body in the barn, George leaves for the bunkhouse to get Carlson's pistol. Candy tells the men of May's murder and they form a posse with Curley in the lead. Slim tells George, "There's only one way to get Lennie out of this." George opens his coat to reveal Carlson's pistol and goes to the river where Lennie is hiding.

George tells Lennie to sit down and look out over the river and try to picture their dream place. Lennie says, "I see it, George!" George pulls the trigger, killing Lennie instantly with a bullet to the brain. It is George's final act of love—his greatest sacrifice. The dream and Lennie are both now out of reach of the influences and evil of this world.

Name _____ Date _____

Of Mice and Men

Multiple Choice

Write the letter of the correct answer to each question below.

1. _____ George watches out for Lennie because he: (a) promised Lennie's mother (b) loves him (c) needs him to get jobs on farms (d) owes Lennie a debt (e) a and b

2. _____ George and Lennie go from job to job because (a) George gets restless (b) Lennie gets bored (c) Lennie gets in trouble (d) the harvest ends and they have to move on

3. _____ George and Lennie's dream is: (a) to own a place of their own (b) to have security (c) to raise rabbits (d) to be independent (e) a and b (f) a, b, and d (g) a, b, c, and d

4. _____ At the ranch George and Lennie worked with: (a) Slim, Crooks, Candy, May (b) Slim, Curley, Carlson, May (c) May, Candy, Carlson, Slim (d) Slim, Candy, Carlson

5. _____ The person at the ranch with the most strength and integrity was (a) Slim (b) Carlson (c) Candy (d) Curley (e) May (f) the owner (g) Crooks

6. _____ Many of the characters in *Of Mice and Men* have disabilities, including (a) George (b) Lennie (c) Crooks (d) Candy (e) Curley (f) Carlson (g) a, b, c, and e

7. _____ Candy felt that he should have shot his dog rather than let Carlson do it because: (a) loving something or someone means you take full responsibility (b) he would have used a gentler method of ending the dog's life (c) Carlson was essentially a mean man

8. _____ George lets Candy share in their dream because: (a) Candy has $300 to contribute (b) George feels sorry for Candy (c) Lennie asks him to (d) Candy can do the work while George and Lennie tend the rabbits (e) a and b (f) a, b, and c (g) a, b, c, and d (h) none of the above

9. _____ Lennie likes to: (a) dream about rabbits (b) kill people (c) be scolded (d) pet soft things (e) a and b (f) a and c (g) a and d (h) a, b, and c (i) a, c, and d (j) all of the above

10. _____ Lennie is better off than most of the men at the ranch because: (a) he's bigger (b) he's smarter (c) he's got George (d) he's May's best friend (e) he can leave when he wants to

11. _____ Lennie is dangerous because: (a) he can't reason (b) he's reckless with his fists (c) he sneaks off where George can't find him (d) he's too proud for his own good

12. _____ Curley is dangerous because: (a) he is incapable of loving anyone (b) he is rich (c) he is too strong for his size (d) he is May's husband (e) he likes to be alone

13. _____ Lennie kills May because: (a) he is jealous of the pups (b) he is jealous of Curley (c) he wants her to stop yelling (d) he wants to pet her soft, golden hair

14. _____ George kills Lennie because: (a) he wants his freedom (b) Slim said that it would be best (c) he loves Lennie (d) he doesn't want to go to jail as an accomplice

15. _____ The story *Of Mice and Men* is about: (a) broken dreams (b) the meaning of love (c) the depression of the 1930's (d) running away (e) a, b, and c (f) a, c, and d (g) a and b

Of Mice and Men

Rewriting

Rewrite the letter written by George to the old couple who need to sell their farm. Correct misspellings, grammatical errors, punctuation errors, and usage errors. You may want to rewrite some sentences and eliminate others entirely.

Dear Mr. and Missus Jones,

Me and Lenny should of conttacted you sooner, but we was working on the rode and couldnt. We would like to by you're farm. We was always been lookin for a place we can calls out own, and where we kin raise are own crops and animals. I'm hopin the price aint to high cause we got only $300 now but we should have alot more reel soon a friend of ours is goin in with us so we should of be able to buy the place within 60 monts if its allright i'll send the $300 now to hold the place til we kin git there an sine the papers wont it be nice for you to have you're bills payed up and wont it be nice for us to

We should be comin thru you're area soon. Pleas mak up the neccissary papers and weel sine when we all three get there.

Your's truley,

George Milton

_____

_____

_____

_____

_____

_____

_____

_____

_____

_____

_____

_____

_____

_____

_____

_____

_____

_____

Name _____ Date _____

Of Mice and Men

Subject-Verb Agreement

Making subjects agree with verbs takes some concentration, especially when a descriptive phrase comes between subject and verb.

Circle the correct verb in each sentence below. Remember that a singular subject requires a singular verb, and a plural subject requires a plural verb.

Example: John Steinbeck, who's written many great novels, <u>places</u> his characters in emotional crises, then watches them struggle their way out.

1. The Great Depression, one of the world's most traumatic events, (provides, provide) a background for many of Steinbeck's writings.

2. One of the more entertaining events in the movie *Of Mice and Men* is when George has Lennie (picks, pick) up the grain wagon.

3. The farm hands (travels, travel) into town once a month to spend their pay.

4. Working, eating, and dreaming (constitutes, constitute) most of each man's life on the ranch.

5. May, one of the loneliest characters in the movie, (keep, keeps) in touch with the outside world by talking to anyone she can find.

6. Curley hates all men who even (look, looks) at his wife.

7. George, along with Slim and Carlson, (were, was) among the most "normal" of the characters.

8. Crooks and Candy, who are both old enough to retire, (have, has) no means of supporting themselves other than working at the ranch.

9. George, Lennie, and Candy (plans, plan) to buy a small 10-acre farm of their own.

10. The dream of having rabbits (haunts, haunt) Lennie's sleep.

11. Crooks, along with several of the men on the ranch, (have, has) lost all hope of ever getting his own piece of land.

12. Candy, because of Slim's and Carlson's comments, (decides, decide) to let Carlson shoot Mack, the sheep dog.

13. George and Slim (believes, believe) that shooting Lennie is better than having the men hunt him down and kill him like a wild animal.

14. George, by having Lennie turn away and "see" their farm in his imagination, (make, makes) it easier to pull the trigger and (ends, end) his friend's life.

15. The movie ends as George (walk, walks) off down the road alone, which makes him seem like everyone else in the film.

© 1994 J. Weston Walch, Publisher   49   The Grapes of Wrath *and 24 More Videos*

Of Mice and Men

Essay

George and Lennie often dream of the day when they'll have their own place and can "live off the fat of the land." Even today this is a dream that a lot of people have, and the more complex and technical our world gets, the more people seem to want to get back to the land. Why? What is this longing all about? What is mankind's relationship to the land?

Write a short essay that tells what *you think* people's relationship is to the land. State your opinion, or viewpoint, in the first paragraph. Then support your view with several examples from your own experience and from the lives of your friends and family members.

_____
_____
_____
_____
_____
_____
_____
_____
_____
_____
_____
_____
_____
_____
_____
_____
_____
_____
_____
_____
_____
_____
_____

Of Mice and Men

Answers

Multiple Choice

1. e	5. a	9. i	13. c
2. c	6. g	10. c	14. c
3. g	7. a	11. a	15. g
4. d	8. f	12. a	

Rewriting

Dear Mr. and <u>Mrs.</u> Jones,

<u>Lenny and I</u> should <u>have contacted</u> you sooner, but we <u>were</u> working on the <u>road</u> and couldn't <u>do so</u>. We would like to <u>buy your</u> farm. We <u>have</u> always been <u>looking</u> for a place we can <u>call our</u> own, and where we <u>can</u> raise <u>our</u> own crops and animals.

I'm <u>hoping</u> the price <u>isn't too</u> high <u>because</u> we <u>have</u> only $300 now, but we should have <u>a lot</u> more <u>very</u> soon. A friend of ours is <u>going</u> in with us so we should be able to buy the place within <u>six</u> months.

If <u>it's all right</u>, I'll send the $300 to hold the place <u>until</u> we <u>can get</u> there <u>and sign</u> the papers. We should be <u>coming through your</u> area soon. <u>Please make</u> up the <u>necessary</u> papers, and <u>we'll sign</u> when we get there.

<u>Yours truly,</u>

George Milton

Subject-Verb Agreement

1. provides	4. constitute	7. was	10. haunts	13. believe
2. pick	5. keeps	8. have	11. has	14. makes, end
3. travel	6. look	9. plan	12. decides	15. walks

Essay

Essays will vary.

THE SKY IS GRAY

Author: Ernest J. Gaines
Short Story Title: "The Sky Is Gray"
Director: Stan Lathan

Running Time: 46 minutes
Year: 1980
Format: color

Summary

On a bleak, windy day in rural Louisiana, a black woman named Octavia walks to the fields to chop cornstalks. She is the mother of two sons, Ty and James, and her husband has been drafted to serve in World War II. She has little money and must carry the heavy burden of raising two boys who are growing up in a world that is often brutal and without opportunity for blacks.

Her oldest son, James, is about 12 or 13 years old. He is timid, sensitive, and childish—three characteristics that Octavia sees as threats to his survival. When James catches two birds in his traps, he wants to keep them as pets rather than slaughter them for food. Octavia stabs one bird with a fork, then hands the fork to James. He is sick at the thought, but through his tears, stabs the bird until it is dead.

That night at supper Octavia declares that she and James will go to Bayonne in the morning to get James's bad tooth pulled. James resists, but in the morning boards the bus with his mother who has counted her quarters carefully before departing.

In the dentist's office James is greeted by the groans of a patient and the silence of the waiting customers. A woman asks a preacher sitting next to her why God makes so much suffering in the world. The preacher replies that God's ways are mysterious and are not to be questioned. A young intellectual retorts, "All things should be questioned. God included." In a dramatic scene the preacher slaps the young man across both cheeks and leaves feeling ashamed. The young man says, "The sky is pink. The grass is black. Words don't mean nothing. Only actions count."

The office closes for lunch and Octavia takes her son to the black part of town to a café where she is propositioned by a black man. She pulls a knife and backs herself and James out of the door and into the street. Moments later an elderly white woman invites Octavia and James into her house for some food. Octavia resists but changes her mind when the woman says she has a chore for James in payment for some food—hauling two garbage cans around to the front. James and Octavia eat eagerly of the meal and share their first smile of the day, as if to say, "It's all right. It's not all hate and cleverness. There is kindness. There is sanctuary."

When they leave, Octavia buys 25-cents worth of salt pork from the woman, but the woman wants to give her double her money's worth. Octavia starts to leave. The woman says to wait, and cuts the slab in half. "Your kindness will never be forgotten," Octavia says, and steps out into the raw winter day with her son in tow.

"Put your collar down, Son. You're not a bum. You're a man," Octavia says. James turns his collar down, squares his shoulders, and proudly walks with his mother down the street to the dentist's office. He has learned from her how to face life and its fears—with a pride and a bravery that come from knowing that the world is not divided by lines of black and white as much as by a graying of philosophies and perspectives that brings a common humanity to us all. Kindness can come from any corner; evil too. One senses, as the film ends, that James is several steps closer to the truth, and that this new knowledge will prepare him to survive in a world that may not always wish him well.

52

Name _____ Date _____

The Sky Is Gray

Opinion

Below are several statements, some of which are opinions and some of which are facts based on or taken from the movie *The Sky Is Gray*. Mark the opinions with an **O** and the facts with an **F**. Choose one of the opinions from the list and write it at the bottom of this page. Then write three arguments in support of the opinion that you could use in an essay.

1. ____ James learned that all black people aren't kind and all white people aren't evil.

2. ____ We should question everything in life.

3. ____ If Octavia had been rich, she would have been a completely different person.

4. ____ Octavia loved James.

5. ____ A person is much smarter to live in the country than in the city.

6. ____ Blacks in Bayonne, Louisiana, in the 1940's could exercise none of their civil rights.

7. ____ Octavia felt that to teach James to be a man she had to be stern.

8. ____ By the end of the film, James had a new respect for his mother.

9. ____ Words don't mean anything—only actions count.

10. ____ Communication would be impossible if people didn't agree on the meaning of certain words.

11. ____ It's better to respond to the situations with your "head" rather than your "heart."

12. ____ The best way to live is to disbelieve everything.

13. ____ Octavia believed that if you lose your pride, you lose everything.

14. ____ James was told to keep his eyes straight ahead in order to stay out of trouble.

15. ____ When Octavia called James a man, he believed her.

Opinion

_____

Support

1. _____

_____

2. _____

_____

3. _____

_____

The Sky Is Gray

Character Analysis

Octavia is a character whose complexity and strength are the power behind Ernest Gaines's story. Answer the questions below to get a clearer picture of this woman, who is struggling to raise her son to be a man in a world that wants so much to keep him a "boy."

1. What survival skills does Octavia teach James?

_____

_____

_____

2. How does Octavia show that she is an intelligent woman?

_____

_____

_____

3. How does she demonstrate courage?

_____

_____

_____

4. In what ways is Octavia like the old white woman (storeowner)?

_____

_____

_____

5. What are Octavia's hopes?

_____

_____

_____

6. What are Octavia's fears?

_____

_____

_____

7. Why does she call James a man?

_____

_____

_____

The Sky Is Gray

Setting

Four important settings in *The Sky Is Gray* are listed below. Write briefly what happened and what James learned in each of these settings that helped him become a "man."

1. The farm

   _____

   _____

   _____

   _____

   _____

   _____

2. The dentist's office

   _____

   _____

   _____

   _____

   _____

   _____

3. The café

   _____

   _____

   _____

   _____

   _____

   _____

4. The white woman's store

   _____

   _____

   _____

   _____

   _____

   _____

The Sky Is Gray

Letter

The character James learns much from his mother about how the world works and how he is to conduct himself in it. Pretend you are James, and in a letter to your father, who is away fighting in the army, tell what you learned and what an impact this learning had on you.

Dear Father,

_____

_____

_____

_____

_____

_____

_____

_____

_____

_____

_____

_____

_____

_____

_____

_____

_____

_____

_____

_____

_____

_____

_____

_____

_____

_____

_____

The Sky Is Gray

Answers

Opinion

1. F	5. O	9. O	13. F
2. O	6. F	10. F	14. F
3. O	7. F	11. O	15. O
4. F	8. F	12. O	

Sample:

Opinion: "Words don't mean anything—only actions count."

Support: 1. Words can be considered actions. 2. Words explain actions (why). 3. All thoughts can't be expressed in action alone.

Character Analysis

1. To kill animals for food; to endure pain while getting a job done; to take care of a problem when it arises; to be tolerant of other people regardless of the color of their skin; to be proud of who he is.

2. She is managing the land well, feeding her family on only a few dollars a month; she knows when to speak up and when to keep silent; she knows when to act and how to defend herself; she knows that her example is much more important than her words to James about growing into manhood.

3. She goes into town seeking help for her son where no one knows her or cares about her; she defends herself in the restaurant against an offensive man; she is trying to maintain her dignity in the midst of poverty and oppression.

4. Octavia is proud and self-sufficient; she doesn't want or need charity; she is competent and hardworking.

5. Octavia wants her children to grow up to be unafraid, intelligent, and hardworking; she wants her life to be a model for her children so she does not have to be ashamed of how she raised them.

6. Octavia is afraid she will be overcome by the tidal wave of racism that hovers over her and her family; she's afraid she will start begging for a chance to be a person, rather than demanding it through sheer effort of will.

7. James has comported himself well during the day; he's kept his head; he's understood what he and his mother have gone through and still maintained his self-confidence and pride.

Setting

1. *The farm:* James learned that life is hard and must be faced with courage. He has to kill to eat meat; he has to work the thin soil to get food; and he has to conserve his money and energy in order for the family to survive.

2. *The dentist's office:* James learned that if one stuck to his principles without considering other people's points of view, a person could make a terrible fool of himself. He also learned that he didn't have to fear religion, but could challenge it and still maintain a level of faith and hope.

3. *The café:* He learned that a woman alone is vulnerable in any culture at any time; his mother showed tremendous courage and strength of character as she fought to defend her honor and her person; he came to respect his mother's strength of will. He also learned that color means nothing. It all comes down to soul.

4. *The white woman's store:* He learned that people can be equals if they look at things other than outside appearances. He saw his mother's pride, the pride that was his by "blood" if he were brave enough to claim it.

Letter

Letters will vary.

BARN BURNING

Author: William Faulkner
Short Story Title: "Barn Burning"
Director: Peter Werner

Running Time: 40 minutes
Year: 1980
Format: color

Summary

A boy stares at a mountain of flame that used to be a barn. His father, Abner Snopes, has set it on fire. The boy is transfixed by the horror of the scene and feels that he is living in a nightmare where everything is twisted and violent and mean. But it is more than a bad dream; it is Sarty's life as part of the Snopes family—sharecroppers who live always on the run, driven by the need to escape the law or vigilantes.

After the barn burning the family travels by wagon to town where Abner Snopes is accused of burning Mr. Harris's barn. Mr. Harris had penned up Abner's hog for tearing up his garden; Abner had sent a message via a black hired hand: "Wood and hay can burn," the message read. That night Harris's barn burned. The judge has no recourse but to call Sarty to the stand to testify against his father, but before he goes through with it, he asks Harris, "Do you want me to question this boy?" Harris says no. Neither man wants to put the boy in the painful position of "squealing" on his flesh and blood. "Get out of this country before dark!" the judge says.

At a campsite later that day, Abner takes Sarty (named for Colonel Sartoris, a Confederate colonel in the Civil War) aside and says, "You were gonna tell 'em weren't ya?" Sarty doesn't answer. "Stick with your blood, boy," Abner advises. "And blood will stick with you."

That in a nutshell is Sarty's problem—he wants no Snopes "blood" sticking with him; he wants out. He thinks often of running away, but he has an innate allegiance to the family and believes that someday his father will change. But Abner Snopes has no intention of altering his method of administering "justice."

The next stop for the Snopes family is a plantation owned by Major De Spain, a rich, landed farmer. Abner goes to De Spain's house to "talk to the man who will own me body and soul for the next eight months." But Abner's goal is not to talk, but to begin another battle in his private war against humanity.

He tracks mud on Major De Spain's rug, and when the Major drops the rug off at Abner's place to be cleaned, Abner scrubs the rug with a huge rock, tearing a hole in the center and ruining it. De Spain wants payment—20 more bushels of corn. Abner takes De Spain to court. Abner loses the case and is fined 10 bushels of corn, a $5 penalty against a $100 rug.

After the trial Abner takes Sarty to the blacksmith shop where Sarty overhears that his father deserted Colonel Sartoris in the war and stole and sold horses to both sides in the conflict; that's how he got his bullet wound which has resulted in a permanent limp.

Back at the house Abner sits by Sarty and Sarty's brother and gives them store-bought crackers and cheese. Then he gives Sarty his pocket knife. Sarty smiles and accepts the gift. But what he doesn't realize is that Abner is celebrating his decision to burn De Spain's barn. That night Abner starts pouring oil from the lamps into a coal-oil can and Sarty confronts him. Abner threatens to tie Sarty to a chair, but Sarty's mother agrees to "hold him."

Sarty breaks loose and runs to De Spain's house yelling, "The barn! The barn!" But it is too late. Abner's black form is visible against the flames as he rides back and forth dumping oil on the fire. Sarty collapses on the ground and doesn't wake until morning. When he gets to his feet, he sees his family riding out of the country, their eyes forward, the mules pulling against the traces, as the sun filters through the trees. He is alone now, abandoned as a traitor to the family and to the law they live by—the law of Abner's revenge.

Name _____ Date _____

Barn Burning

True or False and Matching

Mark the true statements below with a plus (+) and the false statements with a zero (0).

1. _____ Abner Snopes continually moves his family because he is restless.

2. _____ Abner Snopes rules his family like a president rules a democracy.

3. _____ Sarty's brother makes a plan with Sarty to get their father to quit burning barns.

4. _____ The Snopes family is poor because they've had a string of bad luck.

5. _____ Abner Snopes was a war hero who was mistreated by the federal government.

6. _____ Abner Snopes isn't as mean as he is bitter about life.

7. _____ Sarty's only hope is to leave the family and go on his own.

8. _____ Major De Spain requires an additional 20 bushels of corn for his rug.

9. _____ Sarty is essentially alone in the family, with no one to help him.

10. _____ Abner Snopes has been burning barns for years.

Draw lines from each character in the left column to the correct quotations in the right column.

11. Abner Snopes

12. Sarty Snopes

13. Blacksmith

14. Major De Spain

15. Blacksmith's friend

16. Judge

"I find against you, Mr. Snopes."

"He got shot stealing horses."

"At least it'll teach you to wipe your feet before comin' into the house!"

"Wood and hay can burn."

"Get out of this country before dark!"

"He's no more to them than a buzzing bee."

"Stick with your blood."

"He's a deserter."

"Ain't so mean, as sour."

The Grapes of Wrath and 24 More Videos

Barn Burning

Short Answer

1. Why is barn burning such a serious offense?

_____

_____

_____

_____

2. What are the real reasons behind Abner Snopes's vengeful acts?

_____

_____

_____

_____

3. How does Sarty live up to his name, "Colonel Sartoris" Snopes?

_____

_____

_____

_____

4. What does Sarty want most out of life? Why does he want this?

_____

_____

_____

_____

5. Abner Snopes believes that Sarty has a defect in his character. What is that defect?

_____

_____

_____

_____

6. What is Abner Snopes's definition of justice?

_____

_____

_____

_____

Name _____ Date _____

Barn Burning

Dependent Clauses

A dependent clause is a group of words that has a subject and a verb, but cannot stand alone as a sentence; it needs an independent clause added in order to make sense.

Complete the dependent clauses below by adding an independent clause which makes a true statement about the movie *Barn Burning*.

Example: Because Abner kept burning barns, <u>the family was always on the move.</u>

1. If Abner hadn't been a tyrant to the family, _____ .

2. Although Sarty loved his family, _____ .

3. When the judge asked Sarty to take the stand, _____
   _____ .

4. Because Sarty had a conscience, _____ .

5. Whenever Abner moved to a new place, _____ .

6. As the first trial with Mr. Harris proceeded, _____ .

7. When the film ends, _____ .

8. After Major De Spain dropped off the rug, _____ .

9. While Sarty was at the blacksmith shop, _____
   _____ .

10. Because Abner had a twisted sense of justice, _____
    _____ .

11. _____ only after Abner threatened to tie Sarty up
    with a rope.

12. _____ when his family drove off
    and left him standing in a field next to the burned barn.

13. _____ although he was warned to
    "stick to his blood."

14. _____ because he wanted to talk
    to the man who would own him "body and soul" for the next eight months.

15. _____ though he has thoughts of
    running away and leaving the family behind.

Barn Burning

Creative Writing

The movie *Barn Burning*, like any good film, leaves a lot of questions to ponder:

What was Abner Snopes's early life like?

What will Sarty's future be like?

Think about these two questions and answer them the best you can on the lines below.

Abner's Past

_____

_____

_____

_____

_____

_____

_____

_____

_____

_____

_____

Sarty's Future

_____

_____

_____

_____

_____

_____

_____

_____

_____

_____

_____

Barn Burning

Answers

True or False and Matching

1. 0
2. 0
3. 0
4. 0
5. 0

6. +
7. +
8. +
9. +
10. +

11. Abner Snopes—"Wood and hay can burn."   "Stick with your blood."

12. Sarty Snopes—"He's no more to them than a buzzing bee."

13. Blacksmith—"Ain't so mean, as sour."

14. Major De Spain—"At least I'll teach you to wipe your feet before comin' into the house!"

15. Blacksmith's friend—"He got shot stealing horses."   "He's a deserter."

16. Judge—"I find against you, Mr. Snopes."   "Get out of this country before dark."

Short Answer

1. A barn holds the crops, tools, and livestock that are essential to a farmer.

2. Abner is bitter about not being rich and respected. He sees his life as a curse and his barn burning as a way of meting out justice to a world that has ignored him.

3. Sarty acts nobly at the end of the story by trying to warn Major De Spain about his barn burning. Sarty is willing to sacrifice his family's acceptance for justice.

4. He wants his family to be normal, to be loving, and to be honest. He has lived the life of a criminal on the run, and the destruction his father has caused has tormented and angered him.

5. Abner sees that Sarty has a tendency to resist the pull of "blood." Sarty could potentially turn on the family and reject their brutal way of life in favor of doing what is right and respectable.

6. Abner defines justice as the means by which he punishes those around him for being prosperous and decent. Justice for Abner is a form of revenge. The world has shunned him and he's going to make them pay.

Dependent Clauses

Possible responses:

1. Sarty wouldn't have felt so oppressed.

2. he had to do what was right in his own conscience.

3. Sarty was torn between telling the truth and lying about his father's crime.

4. he was miserable living with Abner.

5. someone's barn would eventually burn to the ground.

6. the judge refused to make Sarty testify against Abner.

7. Sarty has decided to live alone rather than live dishonestly.

8. Abner scrubbed a hole through it with a rock.

9. he discovered his father was a deserter from the army.

10. many people suffered.

11. Sarty's mother grabbed his arms and held him back

12. Sarty felt a chapter in his life closing

13. Sarty stood against Abner and his twisted sense of "justice"

14. Abner rode over to Major De Spain's house

15. Sarty gets in the wagon and travels to the next place

Creative Writing

Answers will vary.

SOLDIER'S HOME

Author: Ernest Hemingway
Short Story Title: "Soldier's Home"
Director: Robert Young

Running Time: 41 minutes
Year: 1976
Format: color

Summary

Harold Krebs, a young returning veteran from World War I, finds himself arriving home after the victory parades that greeted his predecessors have ceased. He quietly steps off the train into a world that has gone peaceful. His adjustment is the story of *Soldier's Home*.

Harold wants some time to himself, but his father expects a decision on what kind of work Harold will do, and his mother expects to see gratitude to God for bringing him back safely. Krebs will have none of this; he goes for long walks, sleeps late, and has leisurely breakfasts while he reads the morning paper. On his walks he meets a neighbor who asks about his job prospects at the bank where Harold's father sells real estate. Krebs walks away. At the library he meets his old youth group adviser and walks away from him too. Details of normal living grind away at Krebs. He seems to miss the cruel honesty of the war. He was more alive during the fighting.

One day he meets a fellow veteran, Bill Kenner, who pressures him into going to a dance Friday night. A girl named Roselle teaches Krebs a few dance steps, and when he kisses her, passionately, she leaves him standing alone in the room. "Come back here, Roselle!" he bellows, but she leaves in disgust.

Later, at the car, Bill Kenner is drinking and remembering how terrible the war was, how frightened he was: "I used to stuff my blanket in my mouth so I wouldn't..." he says. Krebs retorts that he wants to remember the good things about the war.

"What good things?" Bill snaps.

"Being a good soldier," Krebs replies. "Doing what you had to do."

"You're crazy!" Bill screams, and stalks off.

On a morning soon after, Krebs is confronted by his mother. She wants him to settle down and get a job. "There are no idle hands in God's kingdom," she says. Krebs broods at his place across the table. "Don't you love your mother, dear boy?" she asks. "No," Krebs replies. "I don't love anybody." His mother breaks down crying and Krebs apologizes. His mother prays for him and asks him if he will pray. "I can't. I can't," he says.

The next morning he packs his bag and leaves for Kansas City. The narrator breaks in: "He had tried to keep his life from being complicated....He had wanted his life to go smoothly. It had just gotten going that way. Well that was all over now, anyway."

Comments: Hemingway gives us a very complex character in Harold Krebs, who comes home from the war a hero in a very personal sense; he has been able to return with his integrity intact. He does not boast in order to laugh off the terror that he knew. He does not throw himself into money-making in order to forget. Krebs, on the contrary, wants to remember. He wants to know about himself, the awfulness of being human as well as the joy in it.

Krebs has found the war to be a surgical operation on his soul, which is now in the process of healing. What was in him was tested to the limit—he killed people, was terrified at times, ignored his religious foundation, and still found a way to live with himself, which is Krebs's greatest victory. He does not have to forget, ignore, or bury what he did, because what he did was his duty; and that, in the end, is what has redeemed him from the atrocity of war.

Soldier's Home

Multiple Choice

Write the letter of the correct answer for each item on the line provided.

1. _____ Harold Krebs comes back from: (a) World War II (b) The Korean War (c) World War I (c) The Spanish-American War (e) none of the above

2. _____ He was wounded in: (a) the chest (b) both legs (c) his right arm (d) his back (e) a and b (f) b and c (g) c and d (h) none of the above

3. _____ When he gets off the train he realizes that: (a) he has missed all the welcome-home celebrations (b) he is alone (c) he is mentally disturbed (d) he must leave his hometown

4. _____ When a neighbor asks Harold about how "bad" it was over there, Harold says: (a) "I was never frightened." (b) "We lost 600 men out of my division." (c) "It wasn't that bad." (d) "I was scared most of the time and am real glad to be back."

5. _____ Harold's behavior is different since he returned from the war; now he: (a) smokes (b) drinks alcohol (c) is rude to many old acquaintances (d) refuses to get a job (e) a and b (f) b and c (g) c and d (h) a, b, c, and d (i) none of the above

6. _____ Harold's father expects the boy to: (a) shape up and get a job (b) see a doctor about his nightmares (c) reenlist in the army (d) stop badgering his little sister who adores him

7. _____ Harold's relationship with his father is: (a) the best it's ever been (b) built on the premise that Harold will meet his father's expectations (c) built on a strong religious foundation (d) weak at this point because Harold has lost faith in his father (e) all of the above

8. _____ Harold wants to remember the "good things" about the war which were: (a) being a good soldier (b) doing what had to be done (c) the wild nights of drinking and carous-ing (d) victory (e) a and b (f) b and c (g) c and d (h) a, b, c, and d (i) none of the above

9. _____ In Harold's view, being a good soldier probably means: (a) not being too afraid to do one's duty (b) killing when it had to be done (c) obeying orders (d) not telling exag-gerated stories of one's exploits in the war (e) a and b (f) a, b, and c (g) a, b, c, and d (h) none of the above

10. _____ Bill Kenner was: (a) Harold's friend (b) a wounded veteran (c) a coward (d) a hero

11. _____ Harold was dissatisfied with Bill Kenner because: (a) Kenner told stories that weren't true (b) Kenner said that the only good in the war was the time they got to spend with the prostitutes (c) Kenner tried too hard to forget about the war (d) Kenner was a deserter (e) a and b (f) a, b, and c (g) a, b, c, and d (h) none of the above

12. _____ Harold's mother didn't understand him because: (a) she saw him as her little boy (b) she was in no way a part of his war experience (c) she believed the stories Bill Ken-ner told (d) she was a fool (e) a and b (f) a, b, and c (g) a, b, c, and d (h) none of the above

13. _____ Harold was angry with his mother because she made him lie about: (a) the war (b) his relationship to his father (c) his love for her (d) his cowardice during the war

Soldier's Home

Short Answer

1. The title *Soldier's Home* suggests a place of rest and recuperation. What is Harold Krebs's home really like? Why do you think the author, Ernest Hemingway, chose this title?

   _____

   _____

   _____

   _____

2. How did the war change Krebs, and what could he do to overcome some of his feeling of alienation?

   _____

   _____

   _____

   _____

3. Harold says that he tried to keep his life from being complicated. What "complications" did he encounter in civilian life? How did he handle these complications?

   _____

   _____

   _____

4. Harold says he wants to remember the "good things" about the war, which are doing what a soldier had to do, and doing it like a soldier should. To what "good things" is Harold referring?

   _____

   _____

   _____

   _____

5. Why does Harold leave home after the scene with his mother?

   _____

   _____

   _____

   _____

6. The name Harold Krebs is plain and simple. Is it representative of the person? Why or why not? Explain.

   _____

   _____

   _____

Soldier's Home

Compare and Contrast

Below are situations in which Harold Krebs found himself telling the absolute truth rather than "fudging the facts." In the first column, write what Harold actually said (paraphrase when necessary). Then in the far right column, write what Harold might have said in place of the blunt truth in the situations presented.

Situation	Harold's Response	Possible Response
1. Krebs's father asks Harold if he learned to smoke in battle.		
2. Krebs's mother says, "Little chance you had to be bored (in the war)."		
3. A neighbor says he has heard that the soldiers had a "mighty difficult time over there."		
4. A boy at the pool hall asks if the reason Krebs is last getting home is because the Army kept the best soldiers behind to keep the Germans in line.		
5. Bill Kenner says, "I was scared. Everybody was scared!"		

Soldier's Home

Projects

Choose one or more of the projects listed below to complete either by yourself or with a small group. Check with your teacher about how the projects are to be handled, and how much time will be allowed for working on them.

#1—Harold Krebs's experience in and reaction to fighting in a war is not that unusual. Many people, both men and woman, who've gone to war have returned changed in some significant ways. Find someone who has been directly involved in a war—a veteran at the local veteran's hospital, a person who was a nurse during a war, an officer, a clerk, a bomber pilot—and interview him or her about not only war experiences, but also his or her experiences upon returning to civilian life. See if your subject will allow you to videotape the interview to play to your classmates. Hold a discussion with the class in which you analyze the similarities and differences between your subject's experiences and Harold Krebs's.

#2—Harold Krebs might have been able to sort out his feelings during and after the war if he'd written about his experience. Writing thoughts on paper allows one to reread and think about them. Write three letters from Harold to three different people in his life. You can invent these people, or assign names to some of those in the film like Harold's old youth group advisor, his little sister, his friend who owned the barber shop, or the girl he danced with named Roselle. Build each letter around a major event that could have happened to Harold over in Europe and which may have had a profound effect on the way he looked at the value of human life, particularly his own life.

#3—Pretend you are Harold and that you've been asked to come to your old high school and speak to the senior class at graduation. Write a speech that you think would reflect Harold's thoughts, and present the speech to your class. Don't read it word for word, but learn it, so you know the content and can say what you mean, using the feelings and emotions that certainly would be the core of such a talk.

#4—Watch the video *Sergeant York,* which is an older film about a real-life war hero, and compare it to *Soldier's Home.* In what ways do the two soldiers deal with their inner conflicts about participating in war? How do the endings of these two films compare? Which one is more realistic? How do you think Harold and Sergeant York would get along? What would they agree on? What would they disagree on? Which film did you like best? Why?

#5—Take an attitude survey in your school about what people think about war—the reasons for it, how it can be avoided, whether it should be avoided, what wars decide, how wars strengthen or weaken a society, how many would enlist and why, what would they fear most and why. When the survey is complete, present your results to the school newspaper staff and see if they will print your article. Then, in your social studies, history, or English class, present the results of your survey, and hold a debate about issues raised.

Soldier's Home

Answers

Multiple Choice

1. c	4. c	7. b	10. b	13. c
2. h	5. h	8. e	11. e	
3. a	6. a	9. g	12. e	

Short Answer

1. Krebs's home life is tense and empty of any meaning for him. He is restless, rootless, and finds that his real home, where he feels most fulfilled, is back in the war with his comrades. Hemingway was pointing out the irony in the typical version of the word "home." Home is where the heart is, even if it is a battlefield.

2. The war has changed Harold beyond his ever coming back to what he was. Life has been so intense for him, that anything less is disturbing to him. He needs to try to understand the distance between himself and the people he talks to. In this way he could eliminate some of the feelings of alienation that plague him.

3. Harold came back to the complicated world of diplomacy. You don't kiss a girl on the first date. You don't wait weeks and weeks to get steady employment. You keep up appearances. Harold rejected these notions and left his family and his hometown.

4. Harold is referring to facing death and dealing out death with a cool head without panic and childlike fear. A good soldier is in "control" of himself under extreme stress. Harold likes that feeling of control and he likes to be where one needs to exert such control.

5. He cannot face the realities he will have to live with if he stays at home. He has questioned his simple faith in God and love and family life; maybe even lost his faith. He needs to find a new way to push himself to the limit as the war did. He can only find this in a place where he is freed from family responsibility and social expectations.

6. Harold Krebs is not simple or mundane in any way. He is extremely complex and aware of what life, through the experience of war, has done to him. His life far outlives the expectations of him which the name Harold would imply.

Compare and Contrast

Harold's Response:

1. "Not really. I just picked it up. We smoked when we were bored."

2. "We were. I was. A lot of the time."

3. "No. Not that bad."

4. Silence—Harold does not answer this question.

5. "That's a lie!"

Projects

Answers will vary.

OUR TOWN

Author: Thornton Wilder
Play Title: *Our Town*
Director: George Schaeffer

Running Time: 120 minutes
Year: 1977
Format: color

Summary

Thornton Wilder's screen-adapted play *Our Town* is built around a narrator, Mr. Morgan, who is also a character in the drama (the drugstore owner). This kindly fellow talks directly to us in the beginning moments of the story, telling us about Grover's Corners—its latitude and longitude, its different types of churches, the names of its oldest families. He then introduces us to the leading families in the film, the Gibbses and the Webbs. We see Myrtle Webb (the newspaper editor's wife) and Julia Gibbs (the doctor's wife) rising early to prepare breakfast for their children (two each), who are getting ready for a typical morning of school.

This "typical" atmosphere is Wilder's framework for the entire film. But he shatters the scenes regularly by having various characters acknowledge the audience by either answering questions, or by being shocked by the audience's presence. The narrator, after the opening domestic scenes, brings in Professor Willard to give a brief geological and anthropological history of Grover's Corners. The professor is nervous before the audience, but proceeds successfully through his speech. Next, Charley Webb, the town newspaper editor, answers questions from an offstage voice about the drinking and culture in the town.

Next we see George Gibbs and Emily Webb, the oldest children of Dr. Frank Gibbs and Charley Webb, talking about school. Emily then goes home and, sitting with her mother, asks if she thinks Emily is pretty enough to attract anybody's attention. Mrs. Webb replies, "You're pretty enough for all normal purposes." Evening falls, and the first snag in the mosaic of Grover's Corners appears: The choir director, Simon Stimpson, is drunk while directing the singing. It's a scandal that has everyone worrying about "how this thing will end."

Three years pass, 1,000 days, and it's July 7, 1904. George and Emily are getting married. Mr. Morgan, our narrator, says that an event as important as this needs some background, so we lapse back to the day George and Emily realized they cared for each other as they talked at the counter in Mr. Morgan's (narrator's) drugstore. The wedding then proceeds with several members of the cast reflecting on the importance and sadness of a wedding day.

The final scene of the film takes place in the graveyard. Emily has just died in childbirth and is standing among all those from Grover's Corners who have died before her—her mother-in-law, Julia Webb; Mr. Stimpson, who hanged himself; Luela Soames, the town gossip; and Emily's brother, Wally, who died of a ruptured appendix.

Emily experiences life from the outside looking in. Memories haunt her, torment her even, to the point that she wants to forget all that happened in her life. Seeing it all and not being able to participate is too painful. In the end she cries out, "I want to live! I want to live!" And she miraculously opens her eyes. She is back in the land of the living, having seen what death really means—the torment of alienation from all things living.

Name _____ Date _____

Our Town

Multiple Choice

Write the letter of the correct answer to each item on the line provided.

1. _____ Grover's Corners is located in: (a) New York (b) Iowa (c) New Hampshire (d) Idaho

2. _____ The title *Our Town* implies that: (a) everyone can identify with certain aspects of life in Grover's Corners (b) only the people in Grover's Corners can be proud of their town (c) foreigners aren't welcome (d) possession is nine-tenths of the law

3. _____ The main characters in the story are: (a) Frank and Julia Gibbs (b) George Gibbs and Myrtle Webb (c) Emily Webb and George Gibbs (d) Charley Webb and Myrtle Webb

4. _____ George Gibbs's goal is to become: (a) a professional baseball player (b) a farmer (c) an engineer (d) a schoolteacher (e) a doctor (f) a newspaper editor

5. _____ Emily Webb shows her practical nature when she says: (a) "I don't care what I wear as long as I look nice." (b) "School is just something you have to go through." (c) "I want to see Paris before I die." (d) "The thing I like most in the world is money."

6. _____ Emily asks her mother if she's pretty and her mother says: (a) "I was pretty and you should be too." (b) "Nobody is pretty unless it's in her soul." (c) "Being pretty is just something you've got to go through." (d) "You're pretty enough for all normal purposes." (e) "No, not like I was when I was your age."

7. _____ Editor Webb tells the audience that in Grover's Corners: (a) there isn't much drinking of alcohol (b) there isn't much culture (c) there's too much traffic (d) a and b (e) a, b, and c

8. _____ The movie *Our Town* is based on four major aspects of human experience: a) school, church, home, and business (b) gossiping, working, studying, and playing (c) birth, daily life, marriage, and death

9. _____ At one point in the story, George breaks down crying while talking to his father because George is: (a) remorseful (b) resentful (c) restive (d) restless (e) angry (f) depressed

10. _____ George and Emily will probably have a good marriage because: (a) they share the same socioeconomic background (b) they knew each other many years before they were married (c) they are both competent, confident people (d) they love each other (e) a and c (f) a, b, and d (g) a, b, c, and d

11. _____ Emily dies during: (a) a car crash (b) childbirth (c) heart surgery (d) a train wreck

12. _____ The surprise ending to the film is that: (a) George Gibbs is dead (b) Julia Gibbs has been dead for years (c) Simon Stimpson kills himself (d) Emily comes back to life (e) the baby survives

13. _____ Emily's most significant statement at the end of the film is: (a) "I can't stand it—the memories are too painful!" (b) "Take me back to the grave!" (c) "I want to live!"

Our Town

Short Answer

1. Today, unlike George Gibbs in 1901, few people dream of becoming farmers. Give three reasons why you think this is so.

_____

_____

_____

2. The narrator says, "Nobody wonderful ever came out of our town, so far as we know." Do you agree or disagree with the narrator? Explain your reasoning.

_____

_____

_____

3. Why do you think the author, Thornton Wilder, had Emily come back to life?

_____

_____

_____

4. Dr. Gibbs said that Simon Stimpson was not cut out for small town life. What does he mean?

_____

_____

_____

5. Why do you suppose most people "climb into the grave married" as the narrator says?

_____

_____

_____

6. Why do you think the author put a narrator into the story who talks directly to the viewer?

_____

_____

_____

7. What is Thornton Wilder's message about the everyday happenings in our lives?

_____

_____

8. Does your view of what happens after death coincide with Thornton Wilder's? Explain.

_____

_____

Name _____ Date _____

Our Town

Extended Metaphor

In the movie *Our Town* Thornton Wilder presents us with an *extended metaphor.* Grover's Corners is like a person with a heart, soul, mind, and body much like any single individual. Think of Grover's Corners (or another town of your choice) and write a brief essay describing it as if it were one individual: What is the brain of the town? What is the heart? What is the lifeblood of the town? What are the arteries? What are the eyes of the town? The ears? The head, hands, and feet? Conclude your essay with a discussion of your metaphorical town's future.

_____

_____

_____

_____

_____

_____

_____

_____

_____

_____

_____

_____

_____

_____

_____

_____

_____

_____

_____

_____

_____

_____

_____

_____

_____

_____

_____

Our Town

Time Line

Like Emily in the movie *Our Town,* you may take for granted events that occur each day in your life. These times would probably take on more importance if you were kept from doing them by illness or injury or (in the movie *Our Town*) by death itself.

Pay attention to some of the simple events that occur during a typical day in your life and note them in the spaces provided below. Then write a brief comment for each event that tells what you would miss if you could not participate in the moment as you do now.

8:00 A.M. _____

_____

_____

_____

10:00 A.M. _____

_____

_____

12:00 NOON _____

_____

_____

2:00 P.M. _____

_____

_____

4:00 P.M. _____

_____

_____

_____

6:00 P.M. _____

_____

_____

_____

8:00 P.M. _____

_____

_____

10:00 P.M. _____

_____

Our Town

Answers

Multiple Choice

1. c	4. b	7. d	10. g	13. c
2. a	5. b	8. c	11. b	
3. c	6. d	9. a	12. d	

Short Answer

Possible answers:

1. (a) Farmland is too expensive nowadays.
   (b) Ninety-eight percent of our population lives in cities.
   (c) There's more interest in high-tech and business professions.

2. The narrator is wrong in the sense that all of the people who come out of Grover's Corners are as complex and wonderful as any people who live in any other town in America. As for fame and fortune, it is probably true that Grover's Corners is not a hotbed of celebrities.

3. Thornton Wilder is making the point that life is more precious than anything we "own." By making Emily come back to life he emphasizes this.

4. Mr. Stimpson is a sensitive soul with fine tastes in the arts. He drinks to dull his senses enough to allow him to exist in a town where great artists, playwrights, and songwriters don't work and live.

5. Most people want to be loved by and committed to something bigger than themselves, and most people seem to choose a family as that "something."

6. The story seems a slice-of-life report with which most people can readily identify.

7. The everyday happenings will only happen once. We are to revere these small moments and appreciate them for what they are: the stuff of life.

8. Answers will vary.

Extended Metaphor

Answers will vary.

Time Line

Answers will vary.

DEATH OF A SALESMAN

Author: Arthur Miller
Play Title: *Death of a Salesman*
Director: Volker Schlondorff

Running Time: 135 minutes
Year: 1986
Format: color

Summary

Death of a Salesman, originally a play by Arthur Miller, is about a 63-year-old traveling salesman whose name, Willy Loman (Low-man), fits him; he is a fumbling, small-time peddler with dreams of being a "big shot." His two sons, Hap and Biff, along with his wife Linda, have suffered under Willy's false dreams and inflated vision of himself all their lives.

In the opening scene Biff and Hap are talking in Hap's room in their parents' home in Brooklyn. Biff has been gone for a year, and for the last three months has had no address; we learn later he's been in jail for stealing a suit. In fact, Biff has stolen himself out of every job he's had since high school. Hap has become a philandering fast-talking hustler who woos women and talks big.

Willy has high hopes for his sons, but his dreams have driven him insane. He hallucinates, has delusions about what was said twenty years ago, and keeps asking the question, "What's the answer?" He'll be sitting at the kitchen table, and suddenly he's out on the porch reliving an afternoon 16 years ago when Biff was a sports star and was about to take on the world.

Biff is dumbfounded at his father's loss of mental stability. He comes downstairs to find Willy out in the garden planting seeds at night. When Biff asks his mother what caused his father's condition, she blames the world, the boys, and Willy's job. "He's a human being. A terrible thing is happening to him, so attention must be paid. He's not to fall into his grave like an old dog." She tells the boys that Willy is trying to kill himself in a car crash and with gas.

Biff promises to get a job and help out. Willy goes to his neighbor, Charlie, and borrows $50 each week so he can pretend he's getting a salary. Biff sets up an appointment with Bill Oliver, a former employer who he believes will stake him for $10,000. Willy is overjoyed.

The next day Willy is fired from the company and he goes to Charlie for a $110 loan to pay his life insurance. "I'm worth more dead than alive," he says. He meets Bernard, Charlie's successful son, and Bernard asks about Biff. Willy cries and asks, "Why'd he lie down, Bernard?" Bernard tells Willy about the time Biff went to Boston to find Willy after he'd flunked math and couldn't graduate. Biff came back shattered. "What happened in Boston, Willy?"

Willy runs out to meet his sons for dinner and when Biff tries to tell him that he was ignored by Bill Oliver and that he stole Bill Oliver's fountain pen on impulse, Willy hallucinates again. He's in Boston in a hotel room with a woman, and Biff comes in. Biff calls Willy a phony, and leaves.

When Biff and Hap come home and find Willy out trying to plant the garden in the dark again, Biff says that he and his dad will have it out. Meanwhile Willy is conversing with the ghost of his brother Ben, telling him he's going to kill himself for the $20,000 policy payoff for Biff's future. Biff brings his dad in the house and tells him he's learned something about himself today. "I'm a dollar-an-hour, Willy!" he screams. "And you're a dime-a-dozen." Willy screams back, and Biff yells, "Will you take that phony dream and burn it before something happens?" Biff hugs his father, kisses him, and goes upstairs, planning to leave in the morning. But Willy, rather than burn the dream, slips out of the house, gets in his car, and kills himself in a car crash.

The final scene is of the family and Charlie at the grave site. "No one das't blame this man," Charlie says. "He had all the wrong dreams," Biff says. "He didn't know who he was." The scene fades as Linda stands over her husband's grave saying, "I paid the last mortgage payment today, Willy. We're free. We're free. We're free."

Name _____ Date _____

Death of a Salesman

True or False and Multiple Choice

Mark the true statements with a plus (+) and the false statements with a zero (0).

1. _____ Willy Loman was a man of integrity.

2. _____ Willy Loman wanted to be known as a kind and humble man.

3. _____ Biff's biggest problem was that he flunked math when he was in high school.

4. _____ Linda Loman stuck by her husband because she loved him.

5. _____ Biff's Uncle Ben taught him how to fight fairly and get ahead in life.

6. _____ Willy Loman encouraged his boys to steal and cheat when they were teenagers.

7. _____ Charley gave Willy $50 a week to keep him quiet about certain business deals.

8. _____ Willy's car accidents were not really accidents at all.

9. _____ At the funeral, Hap said that his father had lived a wasted life.

10. _____ Willy Loman died as he dreamed—the "death of a salesman."

Write the letter of the correct answer on the line provided for each item.

11. _____ Willy Loman sold: (a) silk stockings (b) vending machines (c) insurance (d) tape-recording machines (e) business cards (f) it's never made clear what he sold

12. _____ Willy hallucinates because he: (a) drinks too much (b) is under too much strain (c) can't hold a job (d) can't face reality (e) a and b (f) a and c

13. _____ Biff loses faith in himself when he: (a) loses faith in Willy (b) flunks math (c) gets arrested for stealing (d) runs away from New York (e) none of the above

14. _____ Since Willy's death Hap has decided to: (a) carry on his father's dream (b) set up a casino in Yonkers (c) become a lawyer, like Bernard (d) ask Charley for a loan

15. _____ Willy kills himself because: (a) he can't take any more of the real world (b) he hates and doubts himself (c) he wants to give Biff a $20,000 start in business (d) all of the above

16. _____ Charley offers Willy a job at his firm because: (a) he is sympathetic to Willy's hopelessness (b) they've been neighbors for years (c) he knows Linda Loman will suffer poverty (d) he knows he'll get paid back (e) a and b (f) a, b, and c (g) a, b, c, and d

17. _____ Biff's hope for a new life began when he: (a) turned himself in (b) reconciled with Bernard (c) freed himself from his father's expectations (d) forgave his selfish brother

18. _____ Willy Loman wanted: (a) land (b) an education (c) an appointment (d) fame

Death of a Salesman

Symbols

In literature, as in life, objects sometimes take on a significance that far outweighs the value of those objects in the marketplace; they become symbols that mean something powerful to the characters in the story. Look over the following list of objects that appear in *Death of a Salesman*. Then explain what each object means symbolically to the character(s) involved.

Fountain pen

_____
_____
_____

Football

_____
_____
_____

Garden seeds

_____
_____
_____

Rubber gas hose

_____
_____
_____

Diamond

_____
_____
_____

Silk stockings

_____
_____
_____

Death of a Salesman

Dialogue

Dialogue in any work of art is "tight"; that is, it doesn't include a lot of wasted words about someone's aches and pains, or the condition of the carpeting in the living room, unless such details reveal the personality of the character who's talking.

On the lines below, create a dialogue between Bernard and Biff in which Bernard asks his childhood hero about the trip to Boston that affected Biff so profoundly. Use a style that is swift and sure, as Arthur Miller did in *Death of a Salesman*. Write the dialogue in such a way that Biff, after 16 years, reveals his change of character now that he can see what has happened to Willy, and what he, himself, has become.

Bernard: _____

_____

Biff: _____

_____

Bernard: _____

_____

Biff: _____

_____

Bernard: _____

_____

Biff: _____

_____

Bernard: _____

_____

Biff: _____

_____

Bernard: _____

_____

Biff: _____

_____

Bernard: _____

_____

You may want to practice your dialogue with a partner, then memorize it, and act out this important conversion in front of the class. If you do act it out, be sure to videotape your performance, if possible, because watching yourself is the quickest way to improve and perfect your acting.

Death of a Salesman

Essay

Willy Loman's name is no accident; Arthur Miller gave Willy his name for a reason. What was that reason? Of what significance to the theme of the movie is the name of its main character? How are Willy's futile dreams tied up in his name, Lo-man?

On the lines below write a brief essay explaining the significance of Willy's name to the theme of *Death of a Salesman.*

_____
_____
_____
_____
_____
_____
_____
_____
_____
_____
_____
_____
_____
_____
_____
_____
_____
_____
_____
_____
_____
_____
_____
_____
_____
_____
_____
_____
_____

Death of a Salesman

Answers

True or False and Multiple Choice

1. 0	4. +	7. 0	10. 0	13. a	16. f
2. 0	5. 0	8. +	11. f	14. a	17. c
3. 0	6. +	9. 0	12. d	15. d	18. d

Symbols

Fountain pen—This small object becomes the most valuable piece Biff has ever stolen; it forces him to see how low he's sunk, how petty he's become. The pen is at first a tool of Biff's revenge but ends up being the thing that leads to his liberation from the tyranny of his father's fantastic expectations.

Football—The football symbolizes Biff's life as a success in the Loman household. Biff's athletic ability was to take him far, but his father's weak soul and false values destroyed Biff's faith in everything.

Garden seeds—The seeds represent Willy's lost hopes for burgeoning success. He plants his seeds at night in a place where they cannot grow. Like Willy's dreams, the seeds will die in poor soil, untouched by the light.

Rubber gas hose—Willy's answer to his failed life is expressed in the vile gas hose which he keeps hidden above the water heater. He wants out. He wants to get away from the strange, tormented world he's made for himself.

Diamonds—Diamonds represent the glistening world that is always just out of Willy's reach. Diamonds bespeak adventure. Struggle. Triumph. Success. His brother Ben supposedly discovered such a treasure, which only proved how much more inadequate Willy actually was.

Silk stockings—Willy's faithlessness in the face of a caring, obedient family is symbolized by the silk stockings he gave his girlfriends in the cities where he sold goods. Willy's need for attention and praise could only be bought with cheap stockings; he could not earn such responses from those around him by hard work.

Dialogue

Possible responses:

Bernard: "Biff, I have to say this, you were different after that trip to Boston. Everybody noticed it."

Biff: "Well, I suppose I was."

Bernard: "I mean, you wouldn't talk to people. You wouldn't spend five minutes with me."

Biff: "I remember. It was a long time ago."

Bernard: "But it's always bothered me. What happened? Why'd you throw it all away?"

Biff: "There wasn't much to throw away."

Bernard: "What do you mean? You were great. You had scouts here from big colleges. You were going places!"

Biff: "Ya, well I ended up here. It's been a long journey.

Bernard: "What happened in Boston, Biff?"

Biff: "I found out that my dad was a fake and that he hated my chances of making something of myself."

Bernard: "That's impossible. Your dad worshipped the ground you walked on."

Biff: "That ground turned out to be a grave of buried dreams. But I'm better now. I'm finding out I didn't have to die then. And I don't have to die now."

Bernard: "Who's talking about dying? Biff—what are you talking about?"

Biff: "I'm talking about starting over. About finding out who I am. And I can tell you that it's all back there somewhere in Boston, and I'm here, and I'd like to start up again where we left off."

Bernard: "Well, I've near felt anything different toward you. I was just confused, that's all."

Biff: "I'm glad to hear you say that. I could use somebody to help me see how it really was. Maybe we could have coffee sometime."

Essay

Essays will vary.

ALL QUIET ON THE WESTERN FRONT

Author: Erich Maria Remarque
Play Title: *All Quiet on the Western Front*
Director: Delbert Mann

Running Time: 126 minutes
Year: 1979
Format: color

Summary

The title *All Quiet on the Western Front* comes from a German communiqué sent over the wires at the end of World War I. The message runs across the screen at the end of the film as a bitterly ironic comment on the reasons for the "quiet"—there are hundreds of thousands of men lying face down in the mud, or buried in bomb craters like so much garbage. The protagonist of the film, Paul Bäumer, also succumbs to the "quiet" in the last scene as he is shot while sketching a bird during a lull in the fighting. "We are waiting for the armistice," he said. "We are waiting for peace."

As a German schoolboy Bäumer, at the urging of his teacher, enlists in the infantry. He finds himself at the hands of a sadistic corporal named Himmelstoss, who runs the platoon through mud and endless drills until they avenge themselves with an attack on the corporal the night before they leave for the front.

At the front, the first to be killed is Franz Kemmerich. He is shot in the leg, and the limb is amputated. The platoon visits him, but it is Paul who is there when Kemmerich dies. It is the first in a series of brutal losses that the group suffers as they plod through the war.

The platoon takes comfort from the wisdom and battle skills of one they call "Kat." A displaced shoemaker, Kat is older than the other boys and has a family. He finds food where there is none. He senses shells coming at them and gets them to cover. He teaches them to kill "Frenchies" with a shovel rather than a bayonet. And he makes survivors out of them.

The action is punctuated with Paul Bäumer's narration as he analyzes characters and explains the horrors of killing for self-preservation and for revenge. In a particularly poignant scene, Bäumer stabs a young French soldier in the chest while cowering in a bomb crater. The Frenchman takes hours to die and by the time does, Bäumer is doing everything he can to ease his "comrade's" pain. Paul finds the soldier's wallet with pictures of his French wife and daughter. He realizes that all men are alike, in their families, their fears, and in their pain. When the Frenchman dies, Bäumer says, "I have killed Gérard Duval, the printer."

The change which has been wrought in him is made painfully obvious when he comes home on a 16-day furlough after being wounded. He finds that home has become a strange place. His books are on the shelves, his clothes are in his room, yet he feels cut off from the closest friends he has on earth, the men at the front. He writes his mother a note, then tears it up. She would not understand how he and his world have changed and how he must go to back to those men who give his life meaning. While home he visits his old schoolmaster and tells him that boys should be left to play at being boys. Paul next visits Kemmerich's mother whose son he promised to look out for on the battlefield. He lies to her that her son died instantly without pain. He swears, "May I not return, if he did not die instantly."

Back at the front things take an ominous turn when Paul's comrade Kat is wounded by shrapnel. After carrying the huge man many miles to a dressing station, he finds Kat has been killed with a wound to the head enroute. "We were just talking ten minutes ago," he says. Then the scene switches to the trenches, where Paul is writing to Albert Kropp, one of the original members of the class of 1916 who enlisted with him. He tells Kropp he misses him and lists the numbers of dead, missing, and insane who were part of their group. Only he and Kropp survive. Paul notices a bird perched nearby, and as he did in school, begins to sketch it. But there is the crack of a rifle and a well-aimed bullet cuts him short; he falls into the mud, dead. The message "All Quiet on the Western Front" marches silently across the screen as the film ends.

All Quiet on the Western Front

Multiple Choice

Write the letter of the correct answer to each item on the line provided.

1. _____ From the way the film is made, we would have to conclude that Paul Bäumer: (a) is a ghost speaking from the grave (b) kept a diary (c) wrote a lot of letters to his former teacher (d) wrote and published his own screenplay (e) never really died

2. _____ Bäumer was looked to as a leader by his peers because he was: (a) elected (b) intelligent (c) had common sense (d) mature (e) a and b (f) c and d (g) a, b, and c (h) b, c, and d (i) c and d (j) all of the above (k) none of the above

3. _____ The first of the class of 1916 to die was (a) Detering (b) Mueller (c) Katchinsky (d) Tjaden (e) Kemmerich (f) Bäumer (g) Kropp

4. _____ The boys are first introduced to the brutality of war when they: (a) see Kat die a slow and painful death (b) are cheated by Himmelstoss (c) watch horses die from shrapnel

5. _____ The boys are fortunate to have been assigned to Kat's group because: (a) he fights well (b) he has a nose for finding food (c) he teaches them how to fight (d) he senses danger (e) a and b (f) a, b, and c (g) a, b, c, and d (h) none of the above

6. _____ In the film, Himmelstoss represents: (a) loyalty and power (b) brains and brawn (c) deceit and cowardice (d) stupidity and wealth (e) cunning and strength

7. _____ For entertainment in the dugouts and trenches the boys: (a) played cards (b) killed rats (c) drew birds (d) played Russian roulette

8. _____ The author, Remarque, makes the war intensely personal by: (a) having a soldier narrate the action (b) showing how each soldier has his own personality and his own dreams (c) showing the death of Gérard Duval, the printer (d) showing how the soldiers become emotionally attached to each other (e) a and b (f) a, b, and c (g) a, b, c, and d

9. _____ Before a huge offensive, the French "soften up" the Germans with a major artillery barrage. What does "soften up" mean? (a) The artillery softens the earth by making craters. (b) The exploding shells destroy all vegetation to uncover the German soldiers. (c) The artillery attack is meant to weaken the Germans by keeping them awake and nervous. (d) The artillery shells are meant to gas the Germans, which is the easiest way to kill them.

10. _____ Paul Bäumer says that after a two-day shelling the soldiers are eager to come out of the trenches and fight because: (a) they can avenge themselves (b) they can cause destruction rather than wait to be destroyed (c) they love killing (d) they are afraid (e) a and b (f) a, b, and c

11. _____ When the wind blows, Bäumer says he can smell: (a) blood (b) death (c) destruction

12. _____ The most powerful lesson that Bäumer learned during the war was that: (a) all men are alike (b) war is pointless (c) nobody cares (d) officers are cowards

13. _____ In the last scene, the author wants you to feel: (a) anxiety (b) anger (c) horror (d) fright (e) misery (f) danger (g) love

All Quiet on the Western Front

Creative Writing

People most often commemorate the dead by writing a **eulogy**, an **elegy**, or an **epitaph**. A **eulogy** is a speech of high praise about someone who has died. An **elegy** is a mournful poem telling about the dead person's life. An **epitaph** is an inscription on a tombstone.

Choose one of the characters listed below and write either an elegy or a eulogy about that person. Then on the tombstone, below, write an epitaph that says something brief but accurate about the personality or character of the person buried under it.

Bäumer, Kat, Detering, Kemmerich, Himmelstoss, Kropp

Name _____ Date _____

All Quiet on the Western Front

Symbolism

Two important scenes help reveal the personality of Paul Bäumer. The first is when he's sketching a bird during a lecture by the teacher at school, and the second, when he's sketching another bird on the battlefield in the last scene of the film. The author uses these birds as symbols to "say" something rather than "spell it out" using a lengthy portion of dialogue.

Below are the names of four types of birds. Match each character listed below with a bird, and tell in what ways the bird symbolizes that character. What qualities associated with the bird reveal themselves in the personality of the character? Use a bit of dialogue or a part of a scene involving each character to support and explain your choice of symbol.

Bäumer, Kat, Detering, Kemmerich, Himmelstoss, Kropp

Lark _____
_____
_____
_____
_____

Eagle _____
_____
_____
_____
_____

Hawk _____
_____
_____
_____
_____

Buzzard _____
_____
_____
_____
_____

All Quiet on the Western Front

Letter

One of the most powerful scenes in the film is when Paul Bäumer kills a French soldier, Gérard Duval. Paul vows to write Duval's wife, then decides not to. But what if he had?

Write the letter from Paul to Duval's wife and child. Be sure to include Paul's changed view of life and of the war.

_____

_____

_____

_____

_____

_____

_____

_____

_____

_____

_____

_____

_____

_____

_____

_____

_____

_____

_____

_____

_____

_____

_____

_____

_____

All Quiet on the Western Front

Answers

Multiple Choice

1. b	5. g	9. c	13. c
2. h	6. c	10. e	
3. e	7. b	11. a	
4. c	8. g	12. a	

Creative Writing

Answers will vary.

Symbolism

LARK —Bäumer—Bäumer is symbolized by the lark because of its joyous song and its almost optimistic outlook on life. He was a happy, positive-thinking youth who had a creative spirit which set him apart from ordinary people.

EAGLE—Kemmerich—Kemmerich was brave, loyal, and honest in his last moments on his deathbed. He would not accept Paul's optimistic words about his recovery. The eagle stands for courage and truth which the dying young Kemmerich clearly expresses.

HAWK—Kat—Kat was aggressive in his bid to stay alive, even to the point of brutality in killing his French enemies. Kat hunted the countryside for food, scrounging, killing, and taking what he could in order to survive, and he was skilled at it, as is the hawk.

BUZZARD—Himmelstoss—This ugly creature symbolizes a vile opportunism that is represented in the life and personality of Himmelstoss, the whining, political coward who lives off the death and misery of others. Himmelstoss had a skulking personality, much like that we ascribe to the buzzard.

Letter

Possible answer:

Dear Mrs. Duval,

The horrors of war have escaped none of us. You have suffered the loss of your husband. Your daughter has lost her father. And I have lost myself in this sea of killing and destruction in which I am drowning.

It is with great sorrow and shame that I must confess that I alone am responsible for your husband's death. We met in a bomb crater, me lying there afraid, and he diving in on top of me hoping to avoid shrapnel or a bullet. I panicked and turned and killed him. He died instantly, not knowing what happened. I had to lie next to him for a long time because of the shelling, and as I looked at him I was struck with remorse. I killed him and the war made me do it.

After I found your picture in his wallet, I began to cry. I realized that Gérard was a good man with the same hopes, fears, and pains that I have suffered, that we all are heir to. I am sorry. I will never live this down. Your forgiveness is the only thing that can save me.

I know you hate me, but please try to one day make room for me in your prayers.

Paul Bäumer
150th German Infantry

THE WIND AND THE LION

Writer: John Milius
Director: John Milius

Running Time: 119 minutes
Year: 1975
Format: color

Summary

The film *The Wind and the Lion* is built around a classic triangle: two men in conflict over a woman. However, this triangle deals with world power, intrigue, and love based on deep respect rather than romance.

A desert pirate, El Raisuli the Magnificent, rides into Tangier and kidnaps an American woman named Eden Pedecaris and her two children. He wants gold and guns to provide for the defense of the land he rules (the Riff) against European and Western aggression. But his plan backfires in two ways: first, he has kidnapped a woman of extraordinary courage and intelligence who challenges the Raisuli's thinking and wins his respect; and second, he underestimates the power and brashness of the American government, and especially of its leader, Theodore Roosevelt.

After the kidnapping, President Roosevelt sends a fleet of Marines into Tangier Harbor. The bashaw of Tangier (Arab governor and brother of the Raisuli) is entreated to deal with the Raisuli by the American ambassador, Mr. Gummere. The bashaw refuses. The sultan at Fez (the Raisuli's nephew) will do nothing either.

Meanwhile, Mrs. Pedecaris is learning Arab ways while exchanging challenges with the Raisuli, who keeps her with him as he moves his men across the desert. She plays chess and beats him. She warns him of President Roosevelt's resolve and informs him that Roosevelt shoots a Winchester rifle, which impresses the Raisuli immensely.

Roosevelt is intrigued by the pirate Raisuli and sends him a cable saying: "Pedecaris alive, or Raisuli dead." It is Roosevelt's ambition to not only gain power and land in Morocco, but also prove to this "brigand" that he, Roosevelt, is a formidable foe—a rigorous, manly opponent who would fight face to face if he could.

The American Marines, meanwhile, overrun the palace at Tangier and take the bashaw prisoner. The other foreign governments with ambassadors and soldiers in Tangier (Germans, French, English) are disturbed but do nothing—America has the "big stick" at the moment. The American ambassador offers the Raisuli a deal for the release of Mrs. Pedecaris. The Raisuli accepts, but suspects treachery. And indeed it comes, but not by way of American duplicity. It is the Germans who capture the Raisuli when he rides into a remote village to exchange the woman for guns and gold.

Now with the Marines, Mrs. Pedecaris is troubled, but does nothing. Then, after much thought during the night, she holds a knife to the Marine captain's throat (Captain Jerome) and declares she's going to free the Raisuli from the Germans herself. President Roosevelt promised the Raisuli fair treatment and she's going to see that he gets it. The Marines join her and begin an assault on the Germans. As shots are fired, the Raisuli's men, led by his sheriff, charge the village, routing the Germans. Mrs. Pedecaris finds the Raisuli hanging upside down in a torture chamber and frees him. He says, "We will meet again when we are golden clouds on the wind."

The next scene brings us back to the White House where Theodore Roosevelt is celebrating beneath a huge, stuffed grizzly bear that he shot on one of his hunts along the Yellowstone River. He reads a note from the Raisuli which says, "I am the lion who must remain in my place, while you are the wind and will never know yours."

In the final scene the Raisuli and his sheriff talk at the ocean shore at the foot of the Riff. The sheriff says, "It's all gone. Drifting on the wind. We have lost it all." The Raisuli answers, "Sheriff, is there not one thing in your life worth losing everything for?"

The Wind and the Lion

Multiple Choice

Write the letter of the correct answer to each item on the line provided.

1. _____ In the opening scene, young William Pedecaris thinks he hears: (a) music (b) gunshots (c) an airplane (d) drums

2. _____ The Raisuli kidnaps Mrs. Pedecaris and her children in order to: (a) embarrass the Sultan at Fez (b) get gold and guns (c) get back at the British and Germans (d) protect his interests in Tangier (e) a and b (f) a and c (g) a, b, and c (h) a, b, c, and d

3. _____ Why is the Raisuli surprised at Roosevelt's response to the ransom note? (a) Kidnapping had always worked in the past with the British and other Europeans. (b) He thought President Roosevelt was a political weakling. (c) He figured Roosevelt to be more desperate. (d) He assumed Roosevelt would not use force. (e) all of the above (f) none of the above

4. _____ The Raisuli has the unique gift of being able to: (a) get rich quick (b) make friends of Europeans (c) command respect from all around him (d) kill Germans with impunity

5. _____ Much of the humor in the film derives from Mrs. Pedecaris's: (a) courage (b) intelligence (c) fear (d) stupidity (e) wit (f) a and b (g) a, b, and e (h) c and d

6. _____ President Roosevelt says that the world will never love Americans because they have too much: (a) wealth (b) power (c) greed (d) audacity (e) rapaciousness (f) ebullience

7. _____ President Roosevelt is a very popular man who sees himself as: (a) incompetent (b) deeply afraid (c) alone (d) overworked (e) sheltered from the "real world"

8. _____ At different times, by different people, the Raisuli is referred to as: (a) a brigand (b) a dupe (c) a lout (d) a cold-blooded killer (e) a and b (f) a, b, and c (g) a, b, c, and d

9. _____ The Raisuli shows himself to be all too human when he says: (a) "I am the defender of the faithful." (b) "I am the instrument of God's will." (c) "It's been a bad year; the next one will probably be worse." (d) "I am invincible." (e) a and b (f) a, b, and c (g) none of the above

10. _____ President Roosevelt made a big issue of the kidnapping of Mrs. Pedecaris because: (a) he wanted something bold and brave around which to build his campaign (b) he wanted to use the Atlantic Fleet (c) he hated the Czar of Russia (d) he was at a loss as to what to do with such a complex issue as Arabian politics

11. _____ The source of America's power in the world during the early twentieth century was: (a) good diplomats (b) advanced technology (c) raw courage (d) the Puritan work ethic

12. _____ Mrs. Pedecaris exhibits great courage when she: (a) plots her own escape from the Raisuli (b) threatens to kill the Raisuli if he lays a hand on her (c) takes Marine Captain Jerome as her momentary prisoner (d) rescues the Raisuli from the torture chamber (e) a and b (f) a, b, and c (g) a, b, c, and d (h) a and d (i) a, b, and d

13. _____ The movie *The Wind and the Lion* deals with: (a) love (b) power (c) change (d) respect (e) trust (f) a and b (g) a, b, and c (h) a, b, c, and d (i) a, b, c, d, and e

Name _____ Date _____

The Wind and the Lion

Short Answer

Write a brief answer to the questions below on the lines provided. Use complete sentences.

1. Describe the different ways in which each man, the Raisuli and Theodore Roosevelt, exhibited violent behavior.

_____

_____

_____

_____

2. Tell the story of the Raisuli's imprisonment and of his becoming "Defender of the Faith."

_____

_____

_____

_____

3. Why does Mrs. Pedecaris come to love and respect the Raisuli?

_____

_____

_____

_____

4. Why was kidnapping Mrs. Pedecaris ultimately a serious mistake?

_____

_____

_____

_____

5. What was it that the Raisuli thought worth losing everything for?

_____

_____

_____

_____

6. What was it that President Roosevelt admired about certain of his enemies?

_____

_____

_____

_____

The Wind and the Lion

Letter

The title of the film comes from the last scene in which President Roosevelt sits alone reading a letter from the Raisuli, which states:

> *To Theodore Roosevelt:*
>
> *You are like the wind, and I like the lion.*
>
> *You form the tempest and the sand stings my eyes and the ground is parched.*
>
> *I roar in defiance, but you do not hear.*
>
> *But between us there is a difference: I, like the lion, must remain in my place, while you, like the wind, will never know yours.*
>
> *Mulay Achmed Mohammed El Raisuli the Magnificent, Lord of the Riff, Sultan to the Berbers*

On the lines below, answer the Raisuli's letter as if you were Theodore Roosevelt. Get into the skin of Roosevelt for a moment and determine what he would say. Would he challenge the Raisuli? Threaten him? Praise him? Belittle him? How would Theodore Roosevelt respond?

_____

_____

_____

_____

_____

_____

_____

_____

_____

_____

_____

_____

_____

_____

_____

_____

_____

_____

_____

_____

The Wind and the Lion

Essay

Shortly after Mrs. Pedecaris's capture, the Raisuli tells her a parable. He says, "You see that man at the well—how he draws the water? As one bucket empties, the other fills. It is so with the world. At present you are full of power. But you're spilling it wastefully. And Islam is lapping up the drops as they spill from your bucket."

What did the Raisuli mean? Is he right or wrong? In what ways is he right, or in what way is his logic faulty?

On the lines below, write a brief essay that explains the parable told by the Raisuli and that states and defends your opinion of his assessment of Islam's relationship to the "Europeans."

_____

_____

_____

_____

_____

_____

_____

_____

_____

_____

_____

_____

_____

_____

_____

_____

_____

_____

_____

_____

_____

_____

The Wind and the Lion

Answers

Multiple Choice

1. b	4. c	7. c	10. a
2. e	5. g	8. g	11. b
3. a	6. d	9. c	

Short Answer

1. Roosevelt put up silhouettes of people and shot at them for target practice. He knocked people down with his fists, and had no qualms about sending warships to Tangier. The Raisuli chopped the heads off of two men, shot and sliced several others to death in a raid to free Mrs. Pedecaris. He also had one of his men cut the finger off a woman and send it to Roosevelt.

2. His brother betrayed him and had the Raisuli sent to the dungeons of Magador. There the Raisuli sat for years chained in a cell. He lived through it, won the respect of the guards, and was helped to freedom. He was adopted by a tribe, but had to fight the leader. He killed that man and became Lord of the Riff, Defender of the Faith.

3. He is human, first of all. He boasts before his men, but is not a fake. He is skilled and brave, and he respects Mrs. Pedecaris's rights to privacy and decency. He is impressed by her intelligence and courage. He is loyal to his country and risks his life in its defense continually.

4. The Raisuli challenged the Wind, who responded quickly and violently, using the situation to political advantage. Not only did the Raisuli fight a losing battle, he also lost the land he vowed to hold against all intruders.

5. The chance to defend his sacred homeland against foreign invaders.

6. Their courage in the face of loneliness; their personal commitment to their respective causes; their intelligence and their strength.

Letter

Possible response:

Raisuli,

We differ once again: I do know my place. It is wherever my people are. And were even one of them to be threatened in the land of the lion, I would stir a new storm, drown out your roar, dry up the ground, and swirl sand in your eyes. With every hope that this will not come to pass, I am

Yours in honor,
Theodore Roosevelt

Essay

Essays will vary.

THE GREAT GATSBY

Author: F. Scott Fitzgerald
Novel Title: *The Great Gatsby*
Director: Francis Ford Coppola

Running Time: 151 minutes
Year: 1974
Format: color

Summary

Nick Carraway is invited to the home of his fabulously wealthy cousin, Daisy Buchanan, who lives in East Egg, the exclusive section of Long Island where mansions dot vast green lawns. He has tea with Daisy's husband, Tom, and a woman named Jordan Baker. Tom talks about the white race having to be wary of a takeover by the colored races, and Daisy gabbles on about how happy she is to see Nick.

Nick, who lives in another area called West Egg, has a neighbor named Jay Gatsby. The man is mysterious, handsome, rich, and a thrower of elegant parties. Nick scorns all that Gatsby stands for, but in the end comes to befriend the wealthy romantic whom everyone admires, but mistrusts. Nick meets a third character in this unreal setting—a garage mechanic's wife, Myrtle Wilson, who is Tom's mistress. Tom and Myrtle throw drinking parties for their friends in New York. Nick, the most sensible voice in the story, looks on in amazement and disgust.

One afternoon a man brings Nick an invitation to Gatsby's next party. Nick attends, meets Gatsby, and the next day learns (through Jordan Baker) that Gatsby wants Nick to invite Daisy to tea. It turns out that Gatsby once loved Daisy and wants to rekindle their relationship. "You can't relive the past," Nick says to Gatsby. "Why—of course you can," Gatsby replies.

Daisy spends many afternoons at Gatsby's house and eventually invites him, Nick, and Jordan for lunch. After Tom walks in, Daisy suggests they all go to town, rent five bathrooms at the hotel, and take cold baths. At the hotel Tom confronts Gatsby and asks, "What kind of row are you trying to start in my home?" Gatsby insists that Daisy tell Tom she never loved him and shouldn't have married him. She tries, but fails, and runs out of the hotel. Gatsby follows, and Tom runs after both of them shouting accusations about Gatsby's business deals.

On the way home, Daisy and Gatsby approach George Wilson's gas station in the valley of ashes between the city and Long Island. George's wife, Myrtle, runs out into the road thinking it's Tom who's come to get her and take her away, and Daisy runs her down and drives off. George Wilson is devastated and vows to avenge his wife's murder.

Meanwhile, Jordan, Nick, and Tom arrive at the scene of the accident; Tom believes that Gatsby killed Myrtle and drove off. That night, Gatsby stands in the shadows outside Daisy's home to protect her from Tom. Nick says, "Don't worry. He's not thinking of her right now."

Soon after, George Wilson arrives at the Buchanan mansion. Tom tells the man that the yellow car belongs to Gatsby. Wilson then walks to Gatsby's house, shoots him, then kills himself.

On the day of the funeral Jay Gatsby's father shows up. He's a poor old man who talks highly of his son, Jimmy Gatz, who ran off and got rich. "He was young, but he had brainpower," Mr. Gatz says. After the funeral, Nick and Jordan are having dinner in a hotel lobby and Tom and Daisy appear with eight doormen in tow. "I've been meaning to call, but I've been so busy with the new house," Daisy croons. "Gatsby got what he deserved," Tom snarls. "He ran over Myrtle like a dog in the street." Nick wants to tell him that Daisy killed Myrtle, but says nothing.

"They smash things up, then retreat into their money, or into a vast carelessness or whatever keeps them together," Nick says to Jordan. Later, at home, Nick ponders Gatsby's capacity to pursue romance and nostalgia. He thinks of the first night that Gatsby had seen Daisy's green dock light shining in the dark, and how he must have envisioned things would be. "He did not know that it was already behind him," Nick says, and the film ends.

The Great Gatsby

True or False

Mark the true statements below with a plus (+) and the false statements with a zero (0).

1. ____ Nick Carraway is Daisy's cousin; he is in love with Jordan Baker, Daisy's friend.

2. ____ Gatsby is a drugstore owner who lives in the mansion next to Nick's cottage.

3. ____ Nick meets Gatsby by wandering over to one of his outrageous parties one night.

4. ____ Nick and Gatsby live on the poorer side of Courtesy Bay in West Egg.

5. ____ Gatsby inherited his money from his uncle, the Kaiser of Germany.

6. ____ Tom Buchanan is a wealthy, arrogant racist.

7. ____ Tom likes Myrtle Wilson in the same way that Myrtle Wilson likes her new puppy.

8. ____ Gatsby invites Nick over to his house when he finds out that Nick is Daisy Buchanan's cousin.

9. ____ Jay Gatsby's real name is Jimmy Gatz.

10. ____ Gatsby used to be Daisy's husband before World War I broke out.

11. ____ Gatsby truly believes he can relive the past and marry Daisy and live happily ever after.

12. ____ Daisy said, "Rich girls don't marry poor boys."

13. ____ In this film, Dr. T.J. Eckleburg, the oculist on the billboard, represents God.

14. ____ The rich residents of Long Island must drive through the valley of ashes to get to the city where they make their money.

15. ____ Nick was a hard-nosed realist who believed that anything was possible as long as you had enough money.

16. ____ Nobody likes Nick, because he is originally from the poorer classes.

17. ____ The theme of the movie is: "The love of money is the root of all evil."

18. ____ Tom Buchanan says, "I regret killing Gatsby, but he had it coming to him."

19. ____ Gatsby hates parties, but puts on extravagant bashes in hopes that Daisy will one day wander in as everyone else does.

20. ____ Nick admires Gatsby because love is more important to Gatsby than money.

Name _____ Date _____

The Great Gatsby

Vocabulary

Look up the definitions of the underlined words in Nick Carraway's narration reproduced below. Then write the definitions of these words on the lines provided.

> *In my younger and more <u>vulnerable</u> years my father gave me some advice that I've been turning over in my mind ever since. "Whenever you feel like <u>criticizing</u> anyone," he told me, "just remember that all the people in this world haven't had the advantages that you've had." In consequence, I'm <u>inclined</u> to <u>reserve</u> all my <u>judgments</u>.*
>
> *…It was a golden afternoon and I remember having the familiar <u>conviction</u> that life was beginning over again with the summer. By the autumn my mood would be very different; I would want no more <u>privileged</u> glimpses into the human heart. Only my neighbor, Gatsby, would be <u>exempt</u> from my reaction—Gatsby, who <u>represented</u> everything for which I have an <u>unaffected</u> <u>scorn</u>. For Gatsby turned out all right in the end. It was what <u>preyed</u> on him; what foul dust floated in the wake of his dreams.*
>
> *…At least once a <u>fortnight</u> a <u>corps</u> of <u>caterers</u> came down with several hundred feet of canvas and enough lights to make a Christmas tree out of Gatsby's enormous gardens.*

vulnerable _____

criticize(ing) _____

inclined _____

reserve _____

judgments _____

conviction _____

privileged _____

exempt _____

represent(ed) _____

unaffected _____

scorn _____

prey(ed) _____

fortnight _____

corps _____

caterers _____

The Great Gatsby

Character Study

Nick is the "watcher" in this film; he sees and interprets everything for the viewer, and his relationship to the other characters in the film is that of an observer, a casual participant.

On the lines provided for each character below, write what observations Nick made about that person during the time frame of the film, or what you think his observations would have been if he had kept a diary or journal.

Jordan Baker _____

_____

_____

_____

Daisy Buchanan _____

_____

_____

_____

Tom Buchanan _____

_____

_____

_____

Jay Gatsby _____

_____

_____

_____

Myrtle Wilson _____

_____

_____

_____

George Wilson _____

_____

_____

_____

The Great Gatsby

Essay Questions

On the lines provided, explain these rather strange happenings in the film *The Great Gatsby*.

1. Daisy buries her face in one of Gatsby's expensive shirts and cries.

_____

_____

_____

_____

_____

2. When Nick asks Gatsby about how he makes his money, Gatsby says, "That's my business!"

_____

_____

_____

_____

3. Gatsby throws extravagant parties which he dislikes and refuses to attend.

_____

_____

_____

_____

_____

4. Gatsby puts on his army uniform and dances with Daisy in the candlelight.

_____

_____

_____

_____

5. Gatsby fires his servants and turns out all the lights in his great mansion.

_____

_____

_____

_____

_____

The Great Gatsby

Answers

True or False

1. 0	5. 0	9. +	13. +	17. +
2. 0	6. +	10. 0	14. +	18. 0
3. 0	7. +	11. +	15. 0	19. +
4. +	8. +	12. +	16. 0	20. +

Vocabulary

vulnerable—defenseless, open to attack
criticize—to pass judgment upon something or someone
inclined—to have a tendency; to lean toward
reserve—to save; to store; to hold back
judgments—opinions; decisions
conviction—firm belief
privileged—favored; special
exempt—freed from expected rule or duty
represented—stood for; symbolized
unaffected—genuine, sincere
scorn—disgust; hate; strong dislike
preyed—hunted; stalked
fortnight—two weeks
corps—a group of people
caterers—people who provide food and services at parties

Character Study

Answers will vary. Possible responses:

Jordan Baker—A beautiful woman, very attractive—powerful in her effect upon men. She is bold in her relationships with men and is careless with other people's feelings.

Daisy Buchanan—Daisy is utterly selfish, silly, protected, pampered. She thinks she wants something else, but ultimately enjoys and lusts after money and power. She sees Tom as more of a partner than a husband. They love money together.

Tom Buchanan—Tom is arrogant, wicked, stupid in his use of money. He collects women as some people collect horses or land. He is racist, brutal, violent, and aloof.

Jay Gatsby—Gatsby believes in romantic, adolescent love and in the eternal beauty of it. He will spend everything to experience love as he believes it to be. He chases after impossible things, like the past, and youth, and Daisy Buchanan.

Myrtle Wilson—Myrtle is a pretty woman from a plain upbringing who might have loved her husband at one time, but who has degenerated into loving herself only. She is impressed with trinkets as a child is impressed with brass bands and Christmas lights.

George Wilson—George is a common working man, who must make a living selling gas to people who drive by, leaving him in the valley to slog along. George loves completely, even stupidly. His identity is dependent on his wife's love for him.

Essay Questions

1. Like a worshipper who has touched the robe of her God, Daisy breaks down and weeps at the wicked extravagance expressed in the shelves upon shelves of imported shirts which Gatsby has purchased. She is so awed by such wealth that she cannot compose herself. She is simply in love with money and what it can do.

2. Gatsby is a poor boy who has made it big by acquiring money through whatever means necessary. He is a mystery to the wealthy population of Long Island who have either inherited their wealth or earned it through corporate means. Gatsby is simply snapping out at Nick like he would to anyone else who asked him the same tiresome question.

3. Gatsby has one goal—to marry Daisy and relive the past that he missed. The parties are a tool to draw her to him, like a moth is drawn to the light. The parties are a ploy, not a celebration. They are one of Gatsby's foolish extravagances in the name of unfulfilled love.

4. To relive the past, a moment which in Gatsby's mind could have happened but didn't, he puts on his uniform and dances with Daisy, his beloved. Gatsby is a wild romantic, and this escapade proves it.

5. In a childish effort to keep his affair with Daisy as private as possible, Gatsby clears the grounds of all other people but himself and his ladylove. Of course, what he has done is to create even more gossip and mystery about himself; this is proven by the appearance one afternoon of a newspaper man at Nick's door inquiring about Gatsby.

1984

Author: George Orwell
Novel Title: *1984*
Director: Michael Radford

Running Time: 115 minutes
Year: 1984
Format: color

Summary

Winston Smith is a man tormented by the demand that society has placed upon him—to deny himself and become a transparent arm of the state of Oceania. He resists because he has a memory, he has passion, and he has the need to reason and understand. In Oceania, only those who lose themselves, their sense of history, their own soul, can avoid being shot.

After an emotional rally for Big Brother, we see Winston in his grey, cold apartment pulling a brick from a wall to get at his diary and pen. He writes, "Even before setting pen to paper I've committed the essential crime that contains all others in itself." This is "thoughtcrime." The true citizens of Oceania don't think; they respond. To think is to exercise one's humanity, and "unpersons" are what Oceania requires, not thinkers. Thinking leads to "ownlife," and ownlife is the enemy of the collective life to which all citizens of Oceania are called.

Winston works in the Ministry of Truth, where he rewrites history to match the predictions and pronouncements of the Inner Party, which controls all aspects of life in Oceania, from marital sex to novels read by the "proles," a subclass of humans who are left to their own devices. Winston is a member of the Outer Party, the worker bees. He attends hate rallies against Oceania's arch-enemy, Goldstein, drinks victory gin, and conserves razor blades.

At lunch one day with his "brothers"—Simes, a language specialist employed to destroy the body of words in the culture, and Parsons—he eyes a dark-haired woman across the room. She later bumps into him and slips him a note: "I love you," it reads. They set up a rendezvous and, as an act of political rebellion, have sexual intercourse.

Soon after, Winston meets O'Brien, a gray-haired, steel-eyed member of the Inner Party, who offers Winston the latest copy of the official party dictionary. Winston takes the book, reads it, and begins to form some solid opinions about things: the purpose of war is not to win, but to continue the war; Goldstein and Big Brother are not real; the future belongs to the proles who will rise up and destroy the hierarchy of Oceanic society.

During a moment of quiet reflection in a room above an antique shop in the prole quarter of London, Winston concludes with Julia that he is doomed. Then a voice speaks from behind a picture: "Put your hands over your heads. Stand back to back but don't touch each other!" The Thought Police arrive, club Julia, and haul both of them off to the Ministry of Love to be "cured."

O'Brien comes to cure Winston of his "insanity," after which Winston will be shot. "It may take a long time," O'Brien says. Winston is placed on the rack and tortured until his memory disappears (he'd had recurring memories of his childhood, his mother, and the war), and until he really cannot say accurately, for sure, whether four fingers held up are actually four, or five or three. "Sometimes it's all of them at once," O'Brien says. "It's whatever the Party wants it to be."

Next Winston is electrically shocked and told to clear his mind of all ideas about Big Brother and the proles and Julia. Winston is taken to Room 101, the place where everyone's greatest fear lurks. Winston fears rats, so a cage of rats is placed near his face, and before O'Brien can turn them loose, Winston screams, "Do it to Julia, not to me!"

In the final scene, Winston publicly confesses and asks only to be shot while his mind is clean. "I love you," he says to the image of Big Brother on the telescreen. And the film ends.

1984

Multiple Choice

Write the letter of the correct answer to each item on the line provided.

1. _____ When people meet on the street in Oceania, they call each other: (a) comrade (b) friend (c) brother and sister (d) fellow traveler (e) a and d (f) a and b

2. _____ The constant updates of chocolate ration increases, improvements in the sewage disposal systems, and the military victories on the Malabar Front are told to the people in order to: (a) make them fearful of the Party's power (b) give them confidence in the government (c) make the people happy about being citizens of Oceania (d) give them opportunities for employment (e) a and b (f) b and c (g) b and c (h) c and d (i) all of the above

3. _____ Winston knows he is doomed from the start because: (a) the telescreen will discover him writing in his journal (b) Julia will inform on him (c) Parson's children will turn him in as a thought criminal (d) just thinking about writing anything original is a thoughtcrime and punishable by death (e) a and b (f) b and c (g) c and d (h) none of the above

4. _____ Winston's flashbacks and memories prove that: (a) he had a past (b) history outside of the Party propaganda did and does exist (c) he was once part of a family (d) his mother was murdered by the party (e) a and b (f) a, b, and c (g) a, b, c, and d

5. _____ Winston says that freedom is: (a) the ability to say that $2 + 2 = 4$ (b) the ability to write one's thoughts without criticism (c) the ability to love whom you choose (d) the ability to vote

6. _____ The Party wants all sexual relationships halted because: (a) such relationships can lead to "ownlife" (b) overpopulation would kill the Party's plans for world domination (c) such relationships are illegal (d) such relationships can weaken the military power (e) a and b (f) a, b, and d (g) none of the above (h) all of the above

7. _____ If Winston Smith had lived in a free, democratic country he probably would have been a: (a) policeman (b) politician (c) doctor (d) newspaper reporter (e) disk jockey

8. _____ When Winston places a piece of brown tape over the picture of someone who appears in one of the papers that come across his desk, it means that: (a) the story has been canceled (b) the person no longer exists (c) the person never did exist (d) the person has been killed in the war

9. _____ The "reeducation" of Winston consists mainly of: (a) physical torture (b) attending political rallies (c) viewing hours and hours of the telescreen (d) reciting Party doctrine

10. _____ Julia is essentially: (a) brave (b) stupid (c) vicious (d) loving (e) insane

11. _____ Julia is a committed member of the: (a) antifreedom league (b) anti-Eurasian league (c) antisex league (d) antidemocratic league (e) anti-Party league

12. _____ When Winston and Julia are "reeducated" they are taught to think: (a) that Big Brother is not a person, but a symbol (b) Big Brother is another name for the party (c) O'Brien is the president of Oceania (d) whatever the Party tells them to think (e) a and b (f) a and c (g) none of the above (h) all of the above

13. _____ In the end, Winston: (a) hates Julia (b) hates O'Brien (c) hates himself (d) loves Big Brother

The Grapes of Wrath and 24 More Videos

1984

Fact or Opinion

Below are statements of both fact and opinion. Mark the factual statements with the letter **F**, and opinions with an **O**. Remember that a fact is something that can be proved—verified by research and experiment. An opinion is a belief or judgment based on what seems to be true.

Example: **Fact:** The nation of Canada uses a parliamentary form of government.
Opinion: Canada's governmental system is the most efficient in the world.

1. _____ Every citizen of Oceania is expected to deny his or her personal identity and become totally devoted to the state.

2. _____ It would be better to be dead than to live in a country like Oceania.

3. _____ Thoughtcrime is always fatal in Oceania.

4. _____ There is no such person as Goldstein.

5. _____ *1984* is the most frightening book ever written.

6. _____ In Oceania, people who disagree with Party policy are considered "sick."

7. _____ There is no real flesh-and-blood person named Big Brother.

8. _____ Winston Smith should have killed the antique shop owner the first time he met him.

9. _____ The government should have painted the buildings in the city bright, happy colors instead of letting everything become gray and dilapidated.

10. _____ The government of Oceania is brutal toward people who think for themselves.

11. _____ No modern-day government could ever become as oppressive as that of Oceania.

12. _____ Losing your soul, your will to live, is worse than losing your life.

13. _____ The countryside is presented as a heavenly, green antidote to the gray city in which the citizens of Oceania live and work.

14. _____ Winston Smith is assigned a number by the government of Oceania.

15. _____ Citizens of the United States are assigned a number by the government; it's called the Social Security Number.

16. _____ Winston Smith often has flashbacks to his past which proves to him that there is such a thing as history.

17. _____ Winston Smith's job is to rewrite history to meet present-day conditions.

18. _____ Tampering with the facts of a news article ought to be illegal.

19. _____ If more books were written by machines, the market for books would increase in our world today, and more people would read rather than watch television.

20. _____ The Party wants to eliminate words in order to reduce the opportunity for individual thought and expression.

1984

Newspeak

The language of Oceania is being altered by specialists whose goal is to reduce the size of the pool of words available to people. Instead of different types of "good," such as: *great, super, fantastic, wonderful, fabulous, incredible, incredible,* and *excellent,* there is only the world *good* intensified by the prefix *plus* or *double-plus.* So something that is "great" would be called *plus-good.* Something that is "super" would be called *double-plus good.* The opposites of these terms would be: *plus bad* and *double-plus bad.*

Below is a list of adjectives we use every day. Write the opposite of the term, and then convert it into "Newspeak," the language of Oceania, by adding the appropriate prefix. The first two have been done for you as examples.

Adjective	Opposite term	Very	Extremely
cowardly	brave	plus brave	double-plus brave
sour	sweet	plus sweet	double-plus sweet
hot			
dry			
poor			
new			
bald			
fat			
ugly			
weak			
loud			
dull			
reckless			
happy			
quick			
tame			

1984

Imagery

Imagery is communication that affects the senses: touch, taste, smell, sight, or sound. In *1984* the images are shocking, frightening, even repulsive. Think of what you saw and felt when Winston slipped a piece of "old news" into the jaws of the portable furnace near his desk: Did you smell the burning paper? Hear the clang of the iron fire door as it slammed shut? Did you sense the finality of it, the violence involved in destroying the truth?

Below are six strong images portrayed in the movie *1984*. Read them and then write about the effect the image had on you—what did you see, smell, taste, touch, or hear that made you feel a certain way? How did the image strike you? What did you learn about life in Oceania from each of these images?

1. The cold, dark eyes of Big Brother appear on the giant screen before the crowd.

_____

_____

_____

2. Winston cleans the sink drain for his neighbor, Mrs. Parsons.

_____

_____

_____

3. Winston sees his mother lying dead in the grass.

_____

_____

_____

4. The green, lighted field of the countryside appears in one of Winston's visions.

_____

_____

_____

5. Winston is stretched out on the rack ready to be tortured.

_____

_____

_____

1984

Answers

Multiple Choice

1. a	5. a	9. a	13. d
2. f	6. a	10. a	
3. d	7. d	11. c	
4. g	8. b	12. d	

Fact or Opinion

1. F	5. O	9. O	13. F	17. F
2. O	6. F	10. F	14. F	18. O
3. F	7. F	11. O	15. F	19. O
4. F	8. O	12. O	16. F	20. F

Newspeak

Possible answers:

Adjective	Opposite term	Very	Extremely
hot	cold	plus cold	double-plus cold
dry	wet	plus wet	double-plus wet
poor	rich	plus rich	double-plus rich
new	old	plus old	double-plus old
bald	hairy	plus hairy	double-plus hairy
fat	thin	plus thin	double-plus thin
ugly	beautiful	plus beautiful	double-plus beautiful
weak	strong	plus strong	double-plus strong
loud	quiet	plus quiet	double-plus quiet
dull	exciting	plus exciting	double-plus exciting
reckless	careful	plus careful	double-plus careful
happy	sad	plus sad	double-plus sad
quick	slow	plus slow	double-plus slow
tame	wild	plus wild	double-plus wild

Imagery

Possible answers:

Big Brother's eyes—The eyes are unfeeling, piercing, as if they can see into your thoughts, as if daring you to oppose the mind behind them. Big Brother's eyes strip you bare of all ambition, hope, or creative thought. They are the eyes of a wicked god.

Sink drain—The gray, foul life of the citizens of Oceania is symbolized by the drain in Mrs. Parson's kitchen. It is a colorless, vile life to which these people are subjected, and any thoughts of or attempts at improving it go down the sewer like so much swill.

Winston's mother—The ultimate violence against the body is portrayed in this scene where an innocent woman's blood is spilled on the grass and draws a pack of rats to feast on her. Caring and love are all treasons in Oceania—crimes that bring torment and death.

The green field—This momentary view of paradise is starkly contrasted to the empty, vapid, and violent life of Oceania. There is life in this green field. There is a power greater than that held by Big Brother. That is nature's attraction for Winston, and his dream often takes him there.

The rack—This horrifying scene, as Winston is being pulled apart, assaults the eyes, ears, and mind of any rational human being. Yet the government of Big Brother smiles on such cruelty in the guise of reeducating people to become mindless victims of the system's will.

Almos' a Man

Author: Richard Wright
Short Story Title: "Almos' a Man"
Director: Stan Lathan

Running Time: 51 minutes
Year: 1976
Format: color

Summary

The central object in *Almos' a Man* is a handgun, the one thing that 15-year-old David Glover believes will gain him instant respect, the kind of respect that is afforded to men not boys. People looking down the barrel of David's gun will be afraid. He will have power over them as adults, both white and black, have had over him all his life.

David is plowing the fields of his employer, Mr. Hawkins, when a gunshot rips the air. David stops Jenny, the mule, and listens. Another gunshot echoes from the woods; Mr. Hawkins is hunting while his field hands do the farm work. David scoops up a few stones and tosses them towards the woods, then swings an imaginary shotgun at a covey of imaginary birds and "gets them all." The men working in the field criticize David for his childish, irresponsible behavior, and David responds by cursing them under his breath: "Field niggers. That's all they are!" he says.

On the way back to the barn, having quit early and done a poor job plowing the sun-baked ground, David concludes that he needs a gun and proceeds to the general store owned by Mr. Joe to get a catalog from which he can order it. Mr. Joe loans him a catalog, but on second thought offers to sell David a revolver of his own for $2. Ecstatic, David runs home and begs his mother to give him the $2 from his pay in order to buy Mr. Joe's revolver.

His mother, Essie, resists at first, but then concedes; David can buy the gun, but he must bring it straight home to Essie who will then give it to her husband, Bob. David promises to do just that, but once he gets the gun, he stays away until late in the day, then hides the gun under his pillow. When Essie comes into his room to get the gun, David tells her

he's got it hidden out by the barn. "I'll bring it to Daddy before he goes to the field in the morning," David says.

But he doesn't. He takes the gun with him to the field and, holding it fearfully away from himself with a shaky hand, fires a shot. The gun flips from his hand, and David bites at a wound to his thumb from the kick of the gun, and Jenny runs off. David chases her down, sees she is bleeding from her side, and bemoans his fate at having shot Mr. Hawkins's mule. After running off and burying the gun, he goes home, telling no one of his dilemma.

In the next scene Mr. Hawkins, the two black farmhands, David, and David's family are gathered beside the mule's grave. When Mr. Hawkins says to David, "Tell them what you told me!", David relates his tale of woe, how the mule went berserk and spun around and fell on the plow, puncturing her side. The farmhands snort in disbelief, and one of them says, "It sure looks like a bullet hole to me."

Essie demands, "Tell 'em, David!"

"Don't, Mamma!" David pleads, but Essie tells of his begging for the $2 and buying the revolver from Mr. Joe. David's father is furious, and Mr. Hawkins charges David $50 for the mule, to be taken out of his pay at $2 per month until the debt is paid. The farmhands laugh, and David's father beats him to the ground, interrogates him about the gun, and insists that he get it and return it to Mr. Joe.

The next day, David digs up the gun, fires four shots to prove he can do it without fear, and runs for the train whose haunting call has filled the background of the film from the beginning. The last scene is of David atop a freight car, holding his gun and smiling as he leaves home.

Name _____ Date _____

Almos' a Man

Multiple Choice

Write the letter of the correct answer to each item on the line provided.

1. _____ As the film opens we are startled by: (a) the call of a loon (b) a train whistle (c) a gunshot (d) the crack of a whip (e) a scream

2. _____ David is chastised in the opening segment of the film because he: (a) broke the plow that Jenny the mule is pulling (b) did a shoddy job plowing the field (c) doesn't have his mind on his work (d) stole $2 from Mr. Hawkins (e) a and b (f) b and c (g) c and d (h) a, b, c, and d

3. _____ David's reaction to the chastisement shows that he: (a) resists correction and authority (b) has a bad temper (c) puts others down to make himself feel better (d) puts himself down to make others feel better (e) a and b (f) a, b, and c (g) a, b, and d (h) a, b, c, and d

4. _____ David's mother, Essie, has Mr. Hawkins give her David's wages because: (a) she believes David isn't worth a full salary (b) Mr. Hawkins won't give wage money to minors (c) she thinks David will spend his wages on foolish things (d) she is afraid of David's father (e) none of the above (f) all of the above

5. _____ David becomes obsessed with the idea of owning a gun because: (a) he's too crazy to "fool with" (b) he is driven by a secret urge to kill (c) he thinks the gun will give him authority (d) he knows it is a dangerous weapon if it gets in the wrong hands

6. _____ One of the repulsive habits David has developed is: (a) stealing (b) overeating (c) arguing (d) lying (e) shooting (f) fighting

7. _____ David shoots the mule because: (a) he hates what she represents in his life (b) he hates Mr. Hawkins (c) he hates his life of work and drudgery (d) he doesn't know how to handle a gun

8. _____ David said that the mule died because: (a) some hunter shot her (b) she fell on the plow (c) she had a stroke while plowing and fell on a stick (d) one of the hired men shot her

9. _____ What does David's father, Bob, say about the boy's character? (a) "He's gone and lost his mind!" (b) "He's a fool!" (c) "He ain't nothin' but a boy, and a hardheaded boy!" (d) "He's got no more sense than the mule he killed!"

10. _____ David decides to run away because: (a) his mother didn't stick up for him by keeping his gun a secret (b) his father beat him and humiliated him in front of others (c) Mr. Hawkins's hired men laughed at him (d) no one treats him the way he wants to be treated (e) a and b (f) a and d (g) a and c (h) a, c, and d (i) a, b, c, and d (j) none of the above

11. _____ If David wanted to be considered an adult, he should have: (a) stayed home and worked off the debt to Mr. Hawkins (b) been truthful with his mother and brought the revolver straight home to her as he promised (c) not been slothful in his work (d) realized that "things" don't make an adult; attitudes do (e) a and c (f) a and d (g) a, b, and c (h) a, b, c, and d

Almos' a Man

Short Answer

1. What could David's mother have done to head off the tragedy of David shooting the mule and running away?

_____

_____

_____

_____

2. What could David's father have done to head off the trouble?

_____

_____

_____

_____

3. What could David have done to make life more pleasant for his parents?

_____

_____

_____

_____

4. Was Mr. Hawkins fair or unfair in dealing with David's mistake? Explain.

_____

_____

_____

_____

5. Did the adults in the story expect too much from David? Defend your answer.

_____

_____

_____

_____

6. What is the most serious mistake David makes? Explain your answer.

_____

_____

_____

_____

Almos' a Man

Vocabulary

Find the definitions of the words listed below. Then write the words on the appropriate line(s) in the sentence.

relent(ed)	**impetuous**	**prevarication**	**mollify**	**chastise(d)**
shoddy	**perverse**	**omnipotent**	**panacea**	**enjoin(ed)**
restive	**castigate(d)**	**penchant**	**ignominy**	**incessantly**

1. At the scene of the mule's burial, David's father _____ him to tell the truth.

2. When David was _____ by the field workers for doing a _____ job of plowing, he cursed them as he walked away.

3. David's having a gun made him feel _____.

4. David's mother, Essie, finally _____ and allowed David to buy the gun.

5. Later she said she did it to _____ the boy after he _____ hounded her about the gun.

6. David though the gun would be a _____ for all his troubles.

7. The boy was _____ and seemed always to be wishing he were somewhere else.

8. One of David's most irritating habits was his _____ for _____.

9. David's father, Bob, said that the boy was immature and _____.

10. When David's father _____ him in front of the hired men and Mr. Hawkins, David felt the _____ of the moment, and right there decided to leave.

11. The decision to run away was silly and _____.

Almos' a Man

Interview

In the four boxes below are the headings **child, adolescent, adult, senior citizen**. Find two people who fit into each category and ask them what they want out of life, or what they would like to "be."

Record their responses in the boxes provided, listing their names if you prefer. Then meet with four or five classmates and compare responses. Are there any similarities? Any desires that seem common to each group? Are you surprised at some of the answers you received? Do some of their responses compare to what *you* want out of life?

CHILD	ADOLESCENT

ADULT	SENIOR CITIZEN

Almos' a Man

Answers

Multiple Choice

1. c	5. c	9. c
2. b	6. d	10. i
3. f	7. d	11. h
4. c	8. b	

Short Answer

Possible responses:

1. First, she could have talked to him about his *real* reasons for wanting a gun. His impetuous, immature nature should have clued her to the fact that David lacks basic understanding of some important issues concerning adulthood. She should have refused to get him the gun and gone herself to purchase the weapon if she felt her husband needed one badly enough.

2. Knowing the boy is immature and "hardheaded" he should have had some long father-to-son talks with David and explained the role of a man in a family and in a community. He should have guided David more, should have given him an opportunity to shoot a gun, or whatever it was David saw as important, under firm supervision.

3. He could have stopped lying. One gets the impression that David has been lying for years about trivial things just to have the experience of holding the truth over his parents' heads. He could have been more patient about becoming an adult, and he could have stayed home and worked off the debt to Mr. Hawkins which his father will now have to pay.

4. Mr. Hawkins was more than fair with David, even though he charged full price for the worn-out mule. Being in the South, David actually got off easily. He could have been arrested, or worse.

5. The adults did expect a lot from David in terms of today's standards for teenage labor. He worked all day in the hot sun with the men and was expected to do well and keep quiet. But for the standard of the times, David was doing what many boys of 15 were doing who were black, poor, and tied to the land.

6. David runs off, which will solve nothing. In fact, his departure will cause him more serious problems than having to pay for a dead mule. His immaturity will undoubtedly lead him into the hands of some experienced ruffians who will use him for their own purposes.

Vocabulary

1. enjoined
2. chastised; shoddy
3. omnipotent
4. relented
5. mollify; incessantly
6. panacea
7. restive
8. penchant; prevarication
9. perverse
10. castigated; ignominy
11. impetuous

Interview

Answers will vary.

(The general notion here is that children want to be teenagers, teens want to be adults, adults want to be comfortably retired, and senior citizens want to be children again and have more time to live.)

THE GLASS MENAGERIE

Playwright: Tennessee Williams
Play Title: *The Glass Menagerie*
Director: Paul Newman

Running Time: 134 minutes
Year: 1987
Format: color

Summary

The Winfield family lives in an apartment in St. Louis, Missouri, during the Great Depression. Tom Winfield (who acts as the external narrator to the play as well as a character in it) works in a warehouse to provide food and shelter for his mother, Amanda, and his crippled sister, Laura. His dream is to have adventures, and since he can't have them, he broods, attends movies, writes poems, and drinks. He feels trapped by his mother's expectations and, though he loves Laura, he wants to be free of her. Laura has a collection of small, glass animal figures that she believes are alive; the animals have feelings and they talk to her and she to them. She can't hold a job, daydreams, plays old phonograph records that her father left behind, and when Amanda pays for typing classes at Rubican's Business College, Laura skips class and walks to the zoo to see the penguins. Laura's mother lives in the past when she was a charming, talkative girl of 16. She now wants Laura to be like her, and when Laura fails, asks, "What are we gonna do, amuse ourselves with a glass menagerie and watch parades go by?" She wants success for both her children, but can't seem to get either one of them out of their dreamworlds.

The crunch comes when Amanda begs Tom to bring home a gentleman caller for Laura. Tom resists, but eventually agrees to ask someone, arriving shortly thereafter with the news that Jim O'Connor, a shipping clerk at the warehouse, is coming to dinner. Amanda makes the announcement to Laura who shudders at the thought of the caller being the same Jim O'Connor whom she loved from a distance in high school. "If it's the same person, I won't be able to come to the table, Mamma," she says.

When Jim O'Connor arrives, Laura faints and has to be carried to the couch in the parlor. Amanda claims it's from overwork; Laura has supposedly spent all day in the kitchen preparing their meal. O'Connor is alarmed, but is soothed back into his chair by Amanda who plies him with dandelion wine. Suddenly, the lights go out, which is no surprise to Tom who has used the light bill money for monthly dues to the merchant marine. After taking the opportunity to hand O'Connor a candelabrum and two glasses of wine, Amanda disappears with Tom into the kitchen.

O'Connor chats with Laura, who asks, "Have you kept up with your singing?"

O'Connor then remembers her from high school and recalls a name he'd given her: "Blue Roses," based on his misunderstanding of a sickness Laura had, called pleurosis. They visit some more, and Laura tells O'Connor about her glass animals, particularly the unicorn, which is her favorite. O'Connor gets Laura to dance with him, and as they dance, they bump into the table knocking the unicorn onto the floor. Its horn is broken. Laura says that now it is like all the other horses, not a freak. O'Connor kisses Laura and then tells her he's engaged. He leaves soon after, but not before Laura hands him the glass unicorn as a parting gift.

Amanda is furious with Tom, who she believes has tricked her and made a fool out of her. Tom says he will leave and Amanda screams after him, "Go to the moon, you selfish dreamer!"

At the end of the film Tom says, "I went farther than the moon since time is the longest distance between two places." He tells of his ramblings from city to city and how he could never escape the haunting memory of his sister.

"Blow out your candle, Laura," he says in the last line. "Good-bye." And he walks out of the apartment building and off the screen.

The Glass Menagerie

Multiple Choice

Write the letter of the correct answer for each item on the line provided.

1. _____ In the opening monologue, the narrator contrasts himself with a: (a) doctor (b) fortune-teller (c) gambler (d) lawyer (e) magician (f) snake charmer

2. _____ The entire story is told as a: (a) melodrama (b) fantasy (c) flashback

3. _____ According to the narrator, Tom Winfield, the only symbol in the play is Jim O'Connor, who represents: (a) Laura's dream (b) Amanda's ex-husband (c) Tom's alter ego (d) that long-delayed, but always expected, thing that we live for (e) a, b, c, and d

4. _____ What means the most to Amanda Winfield is: (a) personal courage (b) personal charm (c) money (d) the ability to understand the full meaning of life (e) a and d (f) c and d

5. _____ Tom spends much of his time: (a) drinking liquor (b) smoking (c) going to the movies (d) writing poetry (e) brooding about lack of adventure (f) a and b (g) a, b, and c (h) a, b, c, d, and e

6. _____ Laura spends most of her life: (a) entertaining gentleman callers (b) visiting with her glass animals (c) typing up assignments for Rubican's Business College (d) arguing

7. _____ Amanda sells subscriptions to *The Ladies' Home Companion* in order to raise money for: (a) Laura's college education (b) Laura's courting expenses (c) her own funeral

8. _____ Amanda fights with Tom much of the time because: (a) Tom is so much like his father (b) she hates Tom (c) she fears Tom (d) she is afraid of dying alone and unloved

9. _____ Laura resembles the glass unicorn in that she is: (a) fragile (b) different from other people (c) pampered and protected from harsh treatment (d) a and b (e) a and c (f) a, b, and c

10. _____ Laura's nickname "Blue Roses" was meant to be humorous, but it also represents her: (a) elegant personality (b) melancholy, delicate character (c) persistent, clumsy limp

11. _____ Amanda tells Tom that he can leave them as soon as: (a) he earns enough money to support her and Laura (b) he gets a promotion in the merchant marine (c) he gets married and finds room for her and Laura at his home (d) he finds Laura a gentleman to marry

12. _____ Jim O'Connor feels that Laura's biggest problem is that she is: (a) deceived (b) crippled (c) self-conscious (d) retarded (e) unattractive (f) antisocial (g) sheltered

13. _____ Jim and Laura bump the table while dancing and break the horn off the unicorn. Laura says that: (a) she'll have it fixed before noon tomorrow (b) she'll pretend the unicorn had his horn removed to be like the other horses (c) she'll forgive him if he kisses her

14. _____ When Jim leaves, never to return, Laura gives him the unicorn because: (a) both Jim and the unicorn are the objects of her secret affections (b) she wants Jim to remember her (c) she wants to thank him for his kind words and attention (d) a and b (e) a and c (f) a, b, and c

15. _____ In the last scene Tom cries when he thinks of (a) lost love (b) Amanda (c) Laura (d) his father

The Glass Menagerie

Essay Questions

The answers to the question below are not "right" or "wrong," but open-ended; any reasonable response is perfectly acceptable. Consider each question carefully, and then write the response that you think best answers each question.

1. In this *memory play* we get the story from Tom the character/narrator in the drama. What aspects of the play could have been warped or altered by Tom's perception of what happened years before in the apartment in St. Louis?

   _____

   _____

   _____

   _____

2. The play opens and closes in the same setting—the abandoned apartment where the Winfields once lived. Why does Tom return here? What is he looking for? What does he want?

   _____

   _____

   _____

   _____

3. What is most frightening about the world Laura has built for herself?

   _____

   _____

   _____

   _____

4. Why didn't Amanda Winfield seek a career for herself to secure her and Laura's future?

   _____

   _____

   _____

   _____

Name _____ Date _____

The Glass Menagerie

Character Quotes

Below are several quotes from the four characters in the film *The Glass Menagerie*. Write the name of the character which matches the quote on the line provided.

Jim   Amanda   Tom   Laura

_____ "If a girl had any sense she would look for a man with character."

_____ "In the eyes of others she is terribly shy and lives in a world of her own."

_____ "All pretty girls are a trap, and all men expect them to be."

_____ "I was always gay and happy as a child!"

_____ "I got strings on me."

_____ "The power of love is tremendous!"

_____ "Glass breaks so easily, no matter how careful you are."

_____ "Go to the moon, you selfish dreamer!"

_____ "Blow out your candle, Laura."

_____ "I'll just imagine that he [unicorn] had an operation and his horn was removed."

_____ "I didn't go to the moon; I went much farther."

_____ "Have you kept up with your singing?"

_____ "I had an inferiority complex 'till I took a course in public speaking."

_____ "I may be disappointed, but I'm not discouraged."

_____ "You babbling old witch!"

_____ "I am bewildered by life."

_____ "I wish you were my sister."

The Glass Menagerie

Projects

#1—Memory Play

Select an incident from your past, something dramatic, something memorable. Write out a sketch of the incident, briefly outlining what happened, when it happened, who was there, and what was said. Then go somewhere quiet and put yourself back in time, into the very scene as it was played out by you and the others involved. Write the dialogue that was spoken, word for word as you remember it, and use brief stage directions in parentheses to help characters move about on your "stage." Then ask some classmates to take on the roles in your memory play, and perform it for the class. Use whatever props and costumes you think will help make the drama come alive.

#2—Essay

In *The Glass Menagerie*, written by Tennessee Williams, Laura lives in a world peopled by small fragile animals that she considers her true friends. They need her; she keeps them beautiful, sets them in places where they get different views of the room, and protects them from injury. She imagines all sorts of things that outsiders can only guess at, and lives apart from the hard, unfeeling world of reality.

Andrew Wyeth, the great American painter, made a painting of a neighbor named Christina who was disabled and who had to live a life extremely different from those around her. He called the painting *Christina's World*, and in it we see a longing, a desperation for a better life.

Examine a copy or a photo of this famous painting. Then write a comparison between Wyeth's message and Tennessee Williams's theme in *The Glass Menagerie*.

#3—Literary Analysis

Write a literary analysis of the bird imagery in *The Glass Menagerie* and see if it can be published in your school's literary magazine. Remember to include all the characters in the play in your essay, but be particularly careful to focus on Laura.

#4—News Report

You are a news anchor for Channel 7 in St. Louis. You have heard of the Winfield family from your friend, Jim O'Connor, and you're curious. You take your camera crew to the abandoned apartment where the Winfields once lived and produce a live segment titled: "Where Are They Now?" Tell the story of the Winfields: how they struggled to find a way of life for themselves in the city; how Tom wrestled with his dreams in the face of reality; how Laura built herself a world that was changed by the compassion of one man, Jim O'Connor. Then interview Jim and get his story—what he's doing now, how he got to his present position, and what he knows about the Winfield family. Conclude with a final statement about life that will stay with your audience long after the news hour ends. Videotape your news story and play it for the class. Use whatever props are necessary to convey the proper mood for your report.

#5—Soliloquy

Tom, who was called "Shakespeare" by Jim O'Connor, speaks a soliloquy at the end of the play that ends with the words: "Blow out your candle, Laura." Compare Tom's soliloquy with Macbeth's famous lines from Act V, Scene 5, of the play *Macbeth*:

> *Out, out brief candle! Life's but a walking shadow, a poor player that struts and*
> *frets his hour upon the stage and then is heard no more.*

Memorize the entire soliloquy of Macbeth in Act 5, Scene 5, and recite it to the class. Then tell how the soliloquy compares to Tom's as spoken in *The Glass Menagerie*.

The Glass Menagerie

Answers

Multiple Choice

1. e	5. h	9. f	13. b
2. c	6. b	10. b	14. f
3. d	7. b	11. d	15. c
4. b	8. a	12. c	

Essay Questions

Possible responses:

1. Tom could have made his case bigger than it was; he may not have been quite as miserable at work or at home as he remembered. Tom's mother may have given him some sensible suggestions which he didn't include in the slice of life we see through his eyes. And Laura may not have reacted as positively to O'Connor's visit as the play depicts.

2. Tom may have returned to the apartment because he needed food and shelter. He may have not known that Amanda and Laura had left. Also, Tom might have returned in an effort to confront the guilt he'd been carrying ever since he left Amanda and Laura alone.

3. The most frightening aspect of Laura's world is her lack of knowledge of the world (reality) and of herself. She does not know what she is capable of; she only knows she is disabled. Her world is also very fragile. Like the glass animals she communicates with, she could shatter in the first collision with the harsher sides of reality.

4. She was raised to be dependent and manipulative. Her life as a Southern belle made her seek others to do her bidding. She would feel "common" if she worked outside the home, standing behind a grocery counter, or sitting at a typewriter in someone's office. Her main goal is to keep her imaginary world intact and to shut out the memory of why her husband really left.

Character Quotes

Amanda—"If a girl had any sense..."
Tom—"In the eyes of others..."
Amanda—"All pretty girls are a trap..."
Amanda—"I was always gay and happy..."
Jim—"I got strings on me."
Jim—"The power of love is tremendous!"
Laura—"Glass breaks so easily..."
Amanda—"Go to the moon..."
Tom—"Blow out your candle..."

Laura—"I'll just imagine..."
Tom—"I didn't go to the moon..."
Laura—"Have you kept up..."
Jim—"I had an inferiority complex..."
Jim—"I may be disappointed..."
Tom—"You babbling old witch!"
Amanda—"I am bewildered..."
Jim—"I wish you were my sister."

Projects

Projects will vary.

20. CITIZEN KANE

Screenplay Writers: J. Mankiewicz and Orson Welles
Director: Orson Welles

Running Time: 120 minutes
Year: 1941
Format: black and white

Summary

The story of the deceased Charles Foster Kane begins with a newsreel about his life, showing his wealth, his power, his ambitions, and his public humiliations. A newspaper crew is viewing the film in hopes of doing an in-depth report on not only the life of Charles Foster Kane, but on the *man*. They are especially curious about the one word that escaped the dying man's lips: "Rosebud."

The story is assigned to a reporter named Thompson. Thompson goes to the William Thatcher Library to read the memoirs of Mr. Thatcher for any references to Charles Foster Kane. He interviews Mr. Bernstein, Kane's manager; Mr. Leland, Kane's only "friend"; and Susan Alexander, Kane's second wife, who is a singer at a club in Atlantic City. The story is presented in flashback as the characters tell what they know of Kane's proud and flamboyant past. The one element common to all testimonies is that Kane loved no one, yet yearned for love from others.

The most important flashback, taken from the memoirs of William Thatcher, shows Kane as a boy on his parents' farm. He is outside playing in the snow, coasting on his sled, throwing snowballs at the sign which hangs over the entrance to his mother's boardinghouse. Inside the house Mr. Thatcher from the bank is formalizing a deal in which Charles will go to live with him and be under his guidance until Charles is 25, when the entire fortune from the Colorado Lode, a gold mine whose title was given to Mrs. Kane by a boarder to pay the rent, comes due. The middle name "Foster" takes on a certain significance at this point.

At age 25 Kane writes his guardian that he wants to run the newspaper *The Inquirer*, and that's all. The rest of his holdings, which make up the sixth largest private fortune in the world, can wait. Kane hires a manager, Mr. Bernstein, and a drama critic, Jedediah Leland, and with these two, builds *The Inquirer* to a circulation of over 600,000. Then Kane marries the U.S. president's niece, Emily Norton, who gives him a son and who watches him go from a defender of the common man's ideals to a creator of ideals for the common man to follow. Kane meets a singer, becomes romantically involved, and then runs for governor. He is about to defeat candidate Jim Gettys, when Gettys discovers Kane's love affair and publishes his findings in fantastic headlines across the country.

Kane is ruined. He divorces Emily Norton and marries Susan Alexander who is billed as a "singer." In an effort to remove the quotes from the word "singer," Kane rebuilds the Chicago Opera House in which Susan performs to crowds who hate the show, the acting, and the singing. Jed Leland, Kane's long-time friend, begins writing a scathing review, falls drunk after a few lines, and collapses. Kane finishes the review as Leland intended and then fires him. Jedediah sends back the severance check of $25,000 and a copy of the Declaration of Principles Kane had penned years before when he promised to support the causes of the poor on the pages of *The Inquirer*.

Kane retreats to Xanadu, his palatial mansion on the Gulf Coast. He fights with Susan, and they break up. Kane soon dies alone, unloved, and bitter. On his deathbed he holds a glass ball that contains a miniature cottage with snow-covered roof. When he breathes his last he says, "Rosebud" and drops the glass ball to the floor.

In the final scene when the mansion is being emptied, the boyhood sled of Charles Foster Kane is tossed into the furnace; the name on the sled is "Rosebud." It bespeaks the days of security, of love, and of peace from which Charles Foster Kane had been separated since he was a child. It symbolizes a time when the man was carefree enough to play and to revel in the play, knowing his mother and father were just steps away in the Kane Boardinghouse. Rosebud goes up in flames, along with the career and reputation of a man once feared for his wealth and power, but who was pitied for his lack of understanding and for his inability to know what it means to love and to be loved.

Name _____ Date _____

Citizen Kane

Multiple Choice

Write the letter of the correct answer to each item on the line provided.

1. _____ Charles Foster Kane was a(n): (a) orphan (b) industrialist (c) newspaper publisher (d) politician (e) editor (f) philanthropist (g) crook

2. _____ Kane's money came from: (a) his father (b) a gold mine (c) newspaper sales (d) William Thatcher (e) Jedediah Leland (f) the people

3. _____ Kane runs *The Inquirer* because: (a) he thinks it is fun to run a newspaper (b) he wants to defend the rights of the underprivileged (c) it's the only business he knows (d) he takes some pleasure in attacking the rich and powerful people of the city (e) a and b (f) a, b, and d (g) a, b, and c (h) a and d (i) b and d (j) a, b, c, and d (k) none of the above

4. _____ Kane loses $1 million per year running *The Inquirer.* At that rate it would take how many years to expend his fortune? (a) 10 years (b) 90 years (c) 35 years (d) 60 years

5. _____ Kane defeats *The Chronicle* and brings the circulation of his paper to just over (a) 100,000 (b) 250,000 (c) 360,000 (d) 400,000 (e) 500,000 (f) 684,000

6. _____ The two people with the most to say about Charles Foster Kane are: (a) Bernstein and Thompson (b) Bernstein and Thatcher (c) Thatcher and Leland (d) Alexander and Bernstein (e) Bernstein and Alexander (f) Thompson and Thatcher

7. _____ The important event in Kane's life that is *not* presented thoroughly on film is: (a) his loss of business in 1929 (b) his marriage to Emily Norton (c) his expulsion from Harvard, Cornell, and Yale (d) the death of his son (e) the loss of his only friend

8. _____ There were many hints during the film that Kane could become: (a) king of Europe (b) governor (c) senator (d) president (e) ambassador (f) secretary of state

9. _____ Kane backed out of his run for governor because he: (a) was blackmailed (b) became ill (c) fell in love with the opposition's daughter (d) was afraid of bankruptcy

10. _____ He built his second wife an opera house because: (a) he wanted to prove to the world that she was a singer (b) he wanted the world to remember him as a philanthropist (c) he wanted a chance to develop a new industry: Opera Television

11. _____ Kane's fondest memory is probably of: (a) his acquisition of *The Inquirer* (b) the day he left home for good (c) his early childhood at home (d) his horse, Trigger

12. _____ All of Kane's money could not provide the one thing he needed most: (a) independence (b) security (c) the ability to love (d) inner strength (e) integrity

13. _____ "Rosebud" was a symbol of: (a) youth (b) innocence (c) love (d) poverty (e) loneliness (f) all of the above (g) a, b, and d (h) a, b, c, and e (i) a, b, and c (j) a and e

Citizen Kane

Short Answer

Explain the significance of the comments listed below made by various characters in the film.

1. Mrs. Kane, to Charley Kane, her son: "You won't be lonely, Charles."

_____

_____

_____

_____

2. Editor Rawlston, to news reporter Thompson: "Rosebud—it'll probably turn out to be a very simple thing."

_____

_____

_____

_____

3. Jedediah Leland, to Kane: "You just want to persuade people that you love 'em so much they ought to love you back!"

_____

_____

_____

_____

4. Susan Alexander Kane, to Charles: "You never gave me anything you ever cared about!"

_____

_____

_____

_____

5. Jed Leland, to Thompson the reporter: "He was disappointed in the world so he built one of his own: an absolute monarchy."

_____

_____

_____

6. Charles Foster Kane on his deathbed: "Rosebud." _____

_____

_____

_____

Citizen Kane

Newspaper Article

Write the story that the reporter Thompson would have liked to write about Charles Foster Kane—an article titled "Rosebud Revealed!" Do *not* include the major events in Charles Foster Kane's life, but instead tell about his humanity, the loss of faith he experienced as a child, and the life of loneliness and bravado that he lived until his death within the walls of Xanadu. Reveal the *man*, not the historical events in his life.

The Chronicle

Rosebud Revealed!

Citizen Kane

Projects

#1—Newsreel

Using a video camcorder, design and produce a newsreel that resembles the one shown during the first several minutes of *Citizen Kane*. Use recent news items clipped from magazines, newspapers, and newsletters as pieces in a "video collage" through which you tell the news in a broad, sweeping voice. You may enlist classmates to play silent parts of certain dignitaries and newsworthy people who will be filmed by the all-seeing eye of your camera. Write up the entire narration for the newsreel and give a copy to your teacher before videotaping and presenting your project.

#2—Publish *The Inquirer*

Invent some sensational headlines that only *Inquirer* readers could appreciate, and write news stories to accompany them. Be sure to use large, bold type for your headlines. (Remember the words of Charles Foster Kane: "Big headlines make big news.") You may want to use photos clipped from other publications, or you may wish to combine certain aspects of a variety of photos to get a shocking effect. If you have access to Pagemaker or some other desktop publishing program, all the better. However you build your *Inquirer*, don't make it too long or too crude. Be careful to avoid attacking anyone in print. Let your instructor preview your work before presenting it to the entire class.

#3—Scavenger Hunt

Invent a story about an object that is of dire importance and a serious mystery. Read the story to the class, but *don't* mention the object by name. Then let each person come up with three or four questions, which you will field and answer as honestly as you can, but giving only the information asked for. Accept 20 questions from the audience, and then ask if anyone has figured out the object. If no one can guess, tell the class that the answer will be printed on a piece of paper somewhere in the school tomorrow morning. The first person to find it gets a week-long vacation at Xanadu.

#4—Drama Review

In the spirit of Jedediah Leland, the *Inquirer*'s drama critic, view videos of several plays (*Streetcar Named Desire*, *Raisin in the Sun*, or *Our Town*, for example) and write a review of either the best or the worst of the group. You might want to read several reviews before writing your own. You can find some of these in your library's copy of *The New York Times*, or in such magazines as *Time* or *Newsweek*. See if you might get your review published in the local newspaper or in the paper your school journalism class publishes.

#5—Newspaper Tour

Check with your teacher (who will have to clear it with the principal) to see if you might set up a field trip to a nearby newspaper office. Call the editorial office of a local paper and ask if tours are given. If so, set up a time, tell how many will be attending, and then visit the newspaper office on your own to lay the groundwork for the class tour. Check to see if someone from each department—news, editorial, sports, advertising, etc.—might be available to talk to the class. Write up an account of your day at the newspaper office and see if your school or town newspaper would be interested in printing it with your byline.

Citizen Kane

Answers

Multiple Choice

1. c	5. f	9. a	13. i
2. b	6. c	10. a	
3. f	7. d	11. c	
4. d	8. d	12. c	

Short Answer

1. This ironic statement is made by Kane's mother, who, in fact, forces loneliness onto her child in return for money; Kane is "sold" in a sense, and that experience makes him what he is—a cruel, lonely man without friends and little, if any, warmth in his life and in his soul.

2. Rosebud, in one sense, is extremely simple, being only a child's toy. But in reality it is a symbol of the complexities hidden in Charles Foster Kane's mind. The search for the meaning of "Rosebud" is as difficult as knowing the man himself.

3. Kane spends millions of dollars trying to cause people to become indebted to him in order that he may feel needed. Since he's lost the most important love of his life, he spends the rest of his years trying to create an artificial replacement through "public service" in the *Inquirer.*

4. Kane has bought her only objects on the market—nothing which has any emotional value. Kane has no ability to love others, so he buys them gifts to keep them satisfied at an arm's length.

5. Kane has the money to insulate himself from all human contact. He doesn't feel that people appreciate all that he's "done for them," so he withdraws and builds the gaudy fortress, Xanadu.

6. Rosebud is a symbol of the love and joy and innocence which was left behind with his mother so many years ago. It is the bitter secret of his heart which, as a lament, escapes his lips as he is dying.

Newspaper Article

(Possible response):

This week a world figure left life's "stage" and took the secret of his obsessive lifestyle with him; or so it seemed to reporters who scoured the halls of Xanadu, Charles Foster Kane's pleasure palace, in search of the meaning of his dying word: "Rosebud."

This reporter has discovered, through the aid of a workman in charge of clearing "junk" from Xanadu, that "Rosebud" is not the name of a secret lover, nor the name of a song, poem, or a household pet; "Rosebud" is the name of Charles Foster Kane's childhood sled.

Workman John Feldman said, "I picked it up and tossed it on the fire with the rest of the stuff and didn't notice 'till I was stepping back that the sled said "Rosebud" on it. Before I could pull it out of the flames, it was burning and I couldn't grab it."

This simple child's toy has turned out to be the answer not only to the riddle of Kane's last words but also to the man himself. The world's richest newspaper publisher was haunted by the image of a toy he played with as a child. His money, his fame, and his power could not bring to him the fullness he knew while playing in his own backyard as a boy.

More than his newspapers, than the Chicago Opera House he built for Susan Alexander, and than Xanadu itself, "Rosebud" is Charles Foster Kane's legacy to the people whose affection he so desperately wanted to acquire.

Projects

Answers will vary.

THE RED BADGE OF COURAGE

Author: Tennessee Williams
Novel Title: *The Red Badge of Courage*
Director: John Huston

Running Time: 69 minutes
Year: 1951
Format: black and white

Summary

Henry Fleming, a young private in the Union Army during the Civil War, is with the 304th Regiment at an encampment where nothing is happening but drills and more drills. As the days wear on, the men are becoming restless. Suddenly word comes that the regiment will march tomorrow, thrilling news to all the men except Henry. He writes a letter to his parents telling them how he hopes they will be proud of their son as he goes into battle, but secretly Henry worries about his fear. "Do you think you'd run?" he asks Jim Conklin, a fellow soldier. "I suppose if everybody got to runnin' I'd run," Jim replies.

The thought haunts Henry as he stands sentry duty that night. As he walks along a riverbank, a voice calls out, "Get out of the moonlight, Yank. You make an easy target. Don't make me give you one of them red badges of courage!" The Rebel sentry across the river has shaken Henry in more ways than he knows. Henry has come frighteningly close to death.

The next morning Henry is nervous as the men take up positions on a hill overlooking the battlefield. The men exchange rough taunts and hollow threats. Then the Rebels fire on them. Henry fires back into the smoke that obscures the sun. The Rebels retreat, but then regroup and throw themselves at the Union Army a second time. This time Henry bolts and runs. "It (the war) was all a mistake," he says to himself.

Later he stumbles upon a Union general who is celebrating the victory that Henry's regiment has just helped secure. Henry's heart sinks. The Union army has carried the day, and he feels ashamed. He imagines what things the men will say to him upon his return to camp.

As he heads back towards his regiment he meets a line of wounded men walking up the road, and he envies them. The narrator says, "He conceived persons with torn bodies to be peculiarly happy." Some of the men ask, "Where you hit, boy?" Henry cannot answer.

Among the wounded men is Jim Conklin whom Henry helps along the road. Then Jim runs off into a field, falls to the grass, and dies. On his way back to his regiment Henry meets Union soldiers running towards him. He grabs one and demands to know what's happening. The soldier clubs Henry with his rifle and runs off. Later that night when Henry finally meets up with his group, he tells Tom Wilson that he's been shot in the head. "You've been grazed by a ball," Tom says. "Raised a queer sort of lump on your head like somebody clubbed you." Henry continues to lie and tells Tom that he was "over on the right" fighting with another regiment.

Soon the men are fighting again, and having bluffed himself into heroism, Henry charges out of the trench and fires at the oncoming Rebels. He is instantly considered brave and daring and is lauded by the lieutenant. Later, as Henry and Tom are at the creek filling their canteens, they overhear a general give the order for the 304th to attack because that regiment is the least important regiment and can be spared for this duty. During the attack, Henry once again charges forth, grabs the flag, and leads the regiment in a rout of the Rebels. The commanding officers praise Henry's efforts and commends young Tom Wilson for "leading the charge." But, in a quiet moment, Henry tells Tom the truth; he'd run away earlier because he was afraid. "I guess confessing is good for the soul," Henry says.

Soon the general rides into camp and orders the men to reassemble for another battle. As they march, Henry notes the beauty of the country and how the birds are singing. "As soon as the smoke clears, they're back at it," he says. The film ends with the men marching down the road toward another fight—another chance to earn a red badge of courage.

The Red Badge of Courage

Multiple Choice

Write the letter of the correct answer to each item on the line provided.

1. _____ Henry Fleming is: (a) a lieutenant in the Union Army (b) a corporal in the Confederate Army (c) a private in the Union Army (d) a sergeant in the Confederate Army

2. _____ When he heard that his regiment was marching, Henry: (a) wrote a letter to his parents (b) became afraid (c) challenged Tom Wilson to a fight (d) asked Jim Conklin if he ever considered running from a battle (e) a and b (f) b, c, and d (g) a, b, and d (h) a, b, c, and d

3. _____ Henry first encounters death when: (a) he sees the Rebels charging (b) he runs out of the trenches and fires at the Rebels (c) he's on sentry duty (d) he runs into a Rebel colonel

4. _____ In the first skirmish Henry stays and fights because: (a) he's brave (b) the Confederates never get close enough to charge (c) he has plenty of bullets and powder

5. _____ During the second fight, when Henry ran away, he didn't realize that: (a) all the regiment had been killed (b) they had already won the battle (c) half the regiment ran off at about the same time (d) the lieutenant had reported him to headquarters

6. _____ When Henry meets a column of wounded Union soldiers he: (a) wishes he had a wound too (b) believes that the wounded seem peculiarly happy (c) helps Jim Conklin (d) dies on the operating table (e) a and b (f) a, b, and c (g) a, b, c, and d

7. _____ On the way back to his regiment Henry: (a) is clubbed by a Union soldier (b) is shot in the head by the Rebels (c) falls and twists his ankle (d) hears about Jim Conklin's death

8. _____ When Henry meets up with Tom Wilson he: (a) faints on the operating table (b) receives his medal of honor (c) gives himself up (d) lies about his head wound

9. _____ As they march toward the next battle Henry: (a) brags about his fighting "over on the right" during his absence in the previous battle (b) tells Porter to shut his mouth and keep marching (c) tells Tom Wilson to shut up and stop whining

10. _____ Tom and Henry's regiment is ordered to attack because (a) they are the only regiment that can be spared (b) they are the best fighters on the Union side (c) their lieutenant is the son of General Winterside (d) they have asked for special duty in the next battle

11. _____ Tom grabs the flag and leads the 304th regiment into battle because: (a) he is making up for his cowardice (b) he has overcome his fear of death (c) he wants all the recognition he can get (d) he is a hero (e) a and b (f) a, b, and c (g) a, b, c, and d

12. _____ When Henry confesses to Tom he is surprised because: (a) Tom is dead (b) Jim Conklin left him his watch (c) Tom says that he ran away too (d) he is alone

13. _____ The "red badge of courage" is: (a) a medal (b) an official badge for bravery (c) a war wound (d) a document signed by the colonel

The Red Badge of Courage

Essay Questions

1. Explain how anger can play a part in achieving the "impossible."

_____

_____

_____

_____

_____

2. Define *morale*; then explain how morale can help people succeed when the odds are stacked against them.

_____

_____

_____

_____

_____

3. Explain how fear, like fire, can hurt you or help you depending on how much of it there is.

_____

_____

_____

_____

4. Tell about a time when you achieved something that you believed was far beyond your capabilities. Who else was involved? What kind of doubts did you have? Did you have a specific strategy to achieve your goal? How did you prepare for the struggle?

_____

_____

_____

_____

_____

The Red Badge of Courage

Point of View

Below are listed several actions performed by Henry Fleming. Decide whether you want to present Henry in a positive light or in a negative light. Then write a paragraph using only the details from the list that support your point of view. Be sure you have a clear topic sentence before you begin listing details.

He shudders when he hears the news that the regiment will march within 24 hours.

He writes his parents a letter saying how he hopes they will be proud of him.

He runs from the second encounter with the Confederates and hides in the woods.

He tells Tom Wilson that he's been shot in the head.

He leaps out of the trench and starts shooting at the Rebels.

He helps his wounded comrade, Jim Conklin, when he meets him on the road.

He lies to the men about fighting "way over on the right" during the second battle.

He picks up the flag and leads his regiment into the attack.

He complains about the generals being lunkheads.

He accepts praise from the general for his bravery and daring.

He holds Tom Wilson's watch for him before the first battle.

He goes back to his regiment after running away.

_____

_____

_____

_____

_____

_____

_____

_____

_____

_____

_____

_____

_____

_____

_____

_____

_____

_____

_____

The Red Badge of Courage

Projects

#1—Role-Playing "The Trial of Henry Fleming"

The colonel is about to recommend Henry Fleming for a medal of honor and a promotion when he hears about Henry's flight during the second engagement of the first battle of the 304th Regiment. The colonel is appalled and demands a full investigation. Pretend you are Henry's defense counsel who will defend him against the charge of "desertion under fire" before the panel of officers at a military hearing. Ask some classmates to play the parts of the prosecuting attorney, the colonel, the jury, Henry Fleming, Tom Wilson, Bill Porter, and the lieutenant. Set up a hearing in the classroom and present both sides of the case. Design a medal to be pinned on Henry if you win your argument.

#2—Report

No event in American history has as much material for investigative reporting as does the Civil War. It was an age when industrialization was taking root, fortunes were being made and lost, and millions of black Americans were held prisoner against their will and made to work the land of the free in states all through the South. Using Civil War magazines, diaries, journals, historical photographs, and texts for references, choose one of the topics listed here, and write a report that you will eventually present orally to your classmates: Civil War nurses, prisoners of war, racism, spies, artillery, photography, famous generals, tactics, surgery, Civil War Navy.

#3—Drama

Write a script that reveals a conversation between Henry Fleming and a new recruit whom Henry discovers hiding in the mess tent when the regiment returns from one of its battles. The new recruit is only 16 years old, fresh off the farm in Indiana. He's a colonel's son with no interest in fighting anyone about anything. The boy has been raised by his rich aunt in Fort Wayne; his mother has been dead since he was 5 years old. After you've written the script, find a classmate to play one of the parts, and you take the other. Then perform this scene for the rest of the class. Be sure to videotape it.

#4—Video Interviews

Ask four to six classmates to play the parts of some of the soldiers in *The Red Badge of Courage*. You are the reporter. You are in the field with the 304th Regiment which is dug in on a hill overlooking a meadow that will become a killing field by morning. Ask the men questions that reveal how they feel about the war, life and death, home, peace, and freedom. Get a friend to help handle the video camera and put these soldiers' responses on tape. Maybe some of the students have access to Civil War clothing or artifacts. If not, you might contact an acting company or university drama department to see if they'd lend you something for the soldiers to wear.

#5—Movie Review

Several good movies about the Civil War have been released over the years: *Glory*, *The Civil War* by Ken Burns (public television special), and others. Check out one of these videos from your local or school library, and write a review of the film. Keep in mind that *The Red Badge of Courage* was made many years ago and the film techniques, language restrictions, and subject matter give the film a completely different character than films made today. Remember to comment on plot, setting, theme, and characterization as you compose your review. When finished, see if the school or local newspaper would be interested in publishing it in the next issue.

The Red Badge of Courage

Answers

Multiple Choice

1. c	5. c	9. a	13. c
2. e	6. f	10. a	
3. c	7. a	11. e	
4. b	8. d	12. c	

Essay Questions

1. Anger can be a driving force behind what we do, particularly if we channel our anger against a foe; this foe, however, need not be a person—it could be a concept like racism or apathy. By getting angry a person can call up reserves of energy that aren't available under normal circumstances when a person is mellow and content.

2. Morale means a general attitude of confidence and goodwill within a person and particularly among a group of people. Morale is important in achieving the "impossible" and in maintaining a high level of interest and involvement once success has been achieved.

3. Too much fear can damage one's performance by blocking activity that normally brings success. If one is convinced that the chances for humiliation by defeat are just too great, then one is likely to do nothing—to not even try. Yet not enough fear can cause a person to become reckless and insensitive. A true balance between fear and audacity is the key to real victory.

4. Answers will vary.

Point of View

Positive:

Henry Fleming, though he acted hastily at times, was essentially an honest and trustworthy character. He knew he had done wrong by running away and felt guilt about it; he had to return to his regiment regardless of the humiliation involved. His compassion and loyalty caused him to want to help Jim Conklin as much as possible, though Jim was essentially beyond help. He formed a close friendship with Tom Wilson, another young recruit, held his watch during the first battle, and later confessed his cowardice to Tom in private. As his guilt and courage asserted themselves, he left the trenches, grabbed the regimental flag, and led the 304th into battle. The colonel later commended Henry for his bravery which Henry, in good conscience, had a hard time accepting.

Negative:

From the start, Henry Fleming showed poor character. His first response to the news of a coming battle was to shudder with fear, then go to his tent and write a self-pitying letter to his parents. He later ran from a battle, lied about where he actually went, then lied some more about the lump on his head which he received from a fellow Union soldier. He complained bitterly about the officers and their decisions and battle plans, and when he finally did confess his cowardice under fire, he didn't tell the whole truth. His act of alleged bravery was a guilt-ridden impulse that could have easily cost him his life at the hands of a Confederate rifleman.

Projects

Answers will vary.

LORD JIM

Author: Joseph Conrad
Novel Title: *Lord Jim*
Director: Richard Brooks

Running Time: 154 minutes
Year: 1965
Format: color

Summary

Jim, a graduate of the British Naval Officers School, has a "greed for adventure" and wants to test his mettle against the sea. He believes that there is nothing he cannot face. While he carries out his daily duties, he imagines himself a hero, saving the captain from mutinies singlehandedly, sailing alone across miles of ocean, wrestling with danger and winning easily.

But on board ship one day, he missteps on a ladder and breaks his foot. He's left in port to mend and after recovering enough to walk, takes a job aboard a filthy, foul-smelling vessel called the *Patna*. During a storm, the *Patna* rams some object and Jim inspects the damage. His imagination runs wild and he pictures the ship and its cargo of 800 Moslem pilgrims sinking below the gigantic, violent waves. Jim abandons ship, leaving the 800 pilgrims to fend for themselves. After the storm quiets, Jim and the unscrupulous crew find the *Patna* securely anchored in port.

Jim presents himself for trial and then leaves in shame for ports unknown. While working for the Stein Import Company, Jim heroically saves a boat-load of gunpowder from exploding because of a fire set by a saboteur. Mr. Stein, the boat's owner, and Jim become partners in a scheme to take gunpowder and rifles to Patusan, a village ruled by a vicious pirate called the General.

Jim takes the powder, but is betrayed by the same saboteur who tried to burn the boat earlier. Jim hides the powder and guns ashore, then blows up the boat. He is captured and tortured by the General, but does not reveal where the powder and weapons are stored. A native girl helps Jim escape, and they, with the elders of the village, plan an armed revolt which results in the General's death. The natives now have the General's treasure, the guns, and the powder with which to maintain their freedom.

Meanwhile, the General's former partner, Cornelius, has escaped and returned downriver to enlist the aid of a Mr. Shomberg and Gentleman Brown, a merciless killer. This malicious bunch heads to Patusan to kill Jim (now called Lord Jim by the natives) and retake the treasure. They arrive during a native festival, kill a native boy in their attack, and are repulsed and forced to retreat to their boat shrouded in night fog and hidden from attack by the villagers.

Jim does not want an attack, and promises the village elders that if anyone is hurt during the negotiations with Brown, Jim will forfeit his life. Brown talks Jim into providing a boat and safe passage, but while Jim is waiting for them to leave, Brown slips back to the temple and tries to rob it of jewels. The village's young native leader is fatally stabbed, and Jim arrives in time to help him load two small cannons with powder and jewels. When the thieves appear, Jim fires the cannons, killing the entire mob with bits of diamonds and rubies from the cannon's muzzle.

Jim decides to stand by his promise and offers his life in exchange for the young man who was stabbed. The young man's father agrees to let Jim go, but only if Jim leaves immediately. Jim argues with Stein, who has become Jim's father figure, to let him do what he must, rather than what he would like to do. The next morning Jim places his hat near the body of the little boy shot early in the conflict, then hands the old man a rifle. Jim walks into the square, looks at the sky, the clouds, the beautiful flowers, and then the old man shoots him.

Jim's body is burned in the native custom, and is thus "purified" by fire.

Lord Jim

Plot Sequence

Number the plot events below in order from 1 (the first event) to 20 (the last event). The first three are done for you as examples.

1. _____ Jim pushes a powder keg into the stockade and blows up the General.

2. _____ Jim agrees to negotiate with gentleman Brown, the hired killer.

3. __1__ Jim misses a step on a ladder aboard ship and breaks his foot.

4. _____ Jim detonates a cannon full of jewels and kills Gentleman Brown and Cornelius.

5. _____ The General tortures Jim in order to get the location of the guns and powder.

6. _____ Mr. Stein tries to talk Jim out of standing in front of a rifle and being shot.

7. _____ Jim is killed and purified by fire.

8. __2__ Jim promises the Moslem leader aboard the *Patna* that he (Jim) will not abandon them.

9. _____ Jim hides the powder and guns in the jungle with the help of a native boy.

10. _____ The native boy is shot by Gentleman Brown's men.

11. _____ Cornelius escapes and returns to enlist Shomberg and Gentleman Brown to kill Jim and retake the treasure.

12. _____ Stein arrives in Patusan to the cheers of the people.

13. _____ Jim stays aboard the gunpowder-filled boat and puts out the fire.

14. _____ The woman frees Jim from the General's chains by switching bodies at a funeral.

15. __3__ Jim jumps off the deck of the *Patna* into a lifeboat.

16. _____ Jim is tried in court for cowardice in the line of duty.

17. _____ A French officer testifies that Jim broke no written law by abandoning the *Patna*.

18. _____ Jim returns to port and the *Patna* is waiting for him safely tied up in port.

19. _____ The natives in chains turn and attack the General's men.

20. _____ Mr. Stein and Jim try to hire a boat from Shomberg to go upriver to Patusan.

Lord Jim

Vocabulary

Look up the definition of each word listed below. Then write the word(s) that best completes each sentence on the line provided. Beneath each sentence write out the full definition of the term used in the sentence.

anonymity	flotsam	inflammable	sabotage(d)	aloof
inquest	ominous	pilgrimage	propound(ed)	devastate(d)

1. Jim kept himself _____ from the hordes of poor people on the streets of Java.

   Definition: _____

2. At the _____ Jim's behavior was put under scrutiny of the British Naval Court.

   Definition: _____

3. The story of Jim begins on a gray, overcast, _____ day.

   Definition: _____

4. Jim said to Stein, "Our situation is highly _____."

   Definition: _____

5. The cargo of the *Patna* was 800 Moslems on a _____ to Mecca.

   Definition: _____

6. After the trial, Jim sought _____ among the nameless _____ in the ports along the China Sea.

   Definition: _____

   Definition: _____

7. Mr. Stein's shipment of powder and guns was _____ by the native spy placed there by the General.

   Definition: _____

8. Jim and the *Patna*'s crew believed that the ship had been _____.

   Definition: _____

9. Mr. Stein _____ the notion to Jim that suicide solves nothing.

   Definition: _____

Lord Jim

Setting

Joseph Conrad used two distinct settings for his story *Lord Jim*. The first major action takes place aboard the ship *Patna*, while the second series of events occur in the village of Patusan (paradise).

In the two sections below, compare the settings of the *Patna* and the village of Patusan in terms of parallels that exist between the two: similar characters and character types, familiar moral dilemmas, and any other similarities you recall that appeared or occurred in both places.

Patna _____

_____

_____

_____

_____

_____

_____

_____

_____

_____

_____

_____

_____

_____

_____

Patusan _____

_____

_____

_____

_____

_____

_____

_____

_____

_____

_____

_____

_____

Name _____ Date _____

Lord Jim

Role-Playing

Joseph Conrad's story of a man embroiled in the struggle of clearing his name of a shameful deed touches us all. None of us can say we have never wished for a second chance to make right something we said or did.

Below is the brief outline for a role-playing exercise in which a person feels badly about something he or she did or said. The person discusses the event with two people who have some influence in his or her life (either positive or negative influence). Choose two classmates to work with you as you write out a clear explanation of what the main character (*A*) did to be so ashamed. Then describe each of the three characters involved in the situation, and finally, write out a few words of dialogue each person might use in a conversation with the main character.

When the outline is complete, decide which classmates will take which part in the role-playing, and present your discussion/conversation to the class. Don't memorize lines as in a play. Ad-lib as needed in order to present a *realistic* discussion about a *real* problem that could easily have occurred in the life of character *A*, a modern-day teenager in your school or community.

Problem: _____

_____

Character *A*: (person who made the "mistake" in question)

Name: _____

Reason for guilt about "mistake": _____

_____

Suggested ways to make things right: _____

_____

Character *B*: (good friend of *A*)

Name: _____

Ways *B* can help: _____

_____

Advice *B* gives *A*: _____

_____

Character *C*: (person most affected by *A*'s mistake)

Name: _____

Explain *C*'s feelings: _____

_____

What does *C* want *A* to do? _____

_____

Lord Jim

Answers

Plot Sequence

1. 13	5. 10	9. 9	13. 7	17. 6
2. 16	6. 19	10. 17	14. 11	18. 4
3. 1	7. 20	11. 14	15. 3	19. 12
4. 18	8. 2	12. 15	16. 5	20. 8

Vocabulary

1. aloof—distant in feeling and removed
2. inquest—judicial investigation
3. ominous—threatening
4. inflammable—easily excited, explosive
5. pilgrimage—a holy journey to a shrine
6. anonymity—lack of individuality; flotsam—the wreckage of a ship
7. sabotaged—deliberately destroyed by a familiar party
8. devastated—destroyed, demolished
9. propounded—presented for consideration

Setting

#1—Aboard the *Patna* Jim encountered the selfish, corrupt Captain Brierly, and his equally repulsive first mate. A native population was present which depended solely on the white men for their safety and survival. When the storm struck the ship, Jim experienced the worst fear he had ever known, and his imagination heightened the fear into panic. He ran from the fear, and abandoned the Moslem pilgrims aboard the *Patna*. As he jumped into the waiting lifeboat of the cowardly crew, he saw the face of the Moslem holy man staring at him with an all-knowing look.

#2—In Patusan (paradise) Jim also encountered a wicked man in power, the General, and his vicious sidekick, Cornelius. Both wanted Jim to abandon his conscience and the native population of Patusan and tell them where he'd hidden the guns he brought to help the people defend themselves. Cornelius said, "Nothing can help them!" (meaning the natives) just as Captain Brierly had said to Jim before the crew jumped ship.

But in Patusan, Jim confronted his fear and didn't "jump ship;" he escaped, rallied the villagers, and helped them defeat the General. When Cornelius returned with the murderer, Gentleman Brown, Jim defended his name and offered his life in exchange for any villagers killed in the fight with Brown. Jim sacrificed himself to keep his word, and thus redeemed himself and entered into "paradise."

Role Playing   Answers will vary.

THE CHINA SYNDROME

Authors: Mike Gray, T.S. Cook, and James Bridges
Book Title: *The China Syndrome*
Director: James Bridges

Running Time: 123 minutes
Year: 1979
Format: color

Summary

Kimberly Wells, a features reporter for KXLA-TV in Los Angeles, California, presents a news report about a singing telegram company. She wants to do "hard news" but is stuck with the "soft" assignments that boost ratings.

While on assignment to film the workings of the nearby Ventana Nuclear Power Plant, she gets caught in an emergency: the entire plant starts shaking and warning buzzers flash. The public relations person for California Gas and Electric Company, Bill Gibson, says not to worry. A simple turbine trip has occurred, which means all turbines have stopped turning—very routine. Jack O'Dell, down in the control room, sees it differently. During the emergency, which was caused by a stuck valve, Jack senses an unexplainable shudder. It bothers him, but he keeps his fears to himself. Meanwhile, Richard the cameraman has secretly filmed the entire incident.

The TV station owner, Don Jackovich, won't allow the tape to be used on the air. Richard argues with Jackovich, but to no avail; the tape will stay locked in the film vault until the Nuclear Regulatory Commission has published its investigation results. Richard steals the film, brings it to experts at Point Conception where CG&E's new nuclear plant is about to go on-line in two weeks. The experts say that the emergency was serious and it almost triggered the "China Syndrome," a disastrous situation in which the core of the reactor heats up and melts through the floor of the plant, theoretically all the way to China.

Kimberly and Richard challenge O'Dell with their new-found information, but O'Dell has other things on his mind. He has found that the X-rays of the welds in most of the plant's structure have been faked and agrees to give his copies of the X-rays to Richard's assistant, Hector Sales. On his way to the hearings, Hector is forced off the road and almost killed. Kimberly calls O'Dell to get to the hearings immediately and testify because Hector has been hurt. O'Dell says, "I understand." And indeed he does. On his way to the plant, he's chased by thugs but makes it through the gate of Ventana just ahead of them. He enters the plant and warns his boss, Herman DeYoung, and his friend, Ted Spindler, to run the plant at 75 percent of full power; there's a weak pump that could burst at any moment.

When no one listens to him, he grabs the security guard's gun, orders everyone out of the room, and requests that Kimberly Wells interview him for television. Kimberly arrives and Richard convinces the chairman of the board of CG&E, Evan McCormack, to let O'Dell have his way before he floods the containment area with radioactivity and destroys the plant.

In the middle of O'Dell's muddled, emotional interview, the warning systems go berserk. Chairman McCormack orders that O'Dell be humored until an emergency can be simulated that will distract O'Dell long enough for a S.W.A.T. team to break in and kill him. The plan works and O'Dell is fatally shot. Just before he dies he whispers, "I can feel it!" Suddenly the plant shakes violently and the lights go black; the weak pump breaks apart and the plant shuts down.

Outside, camera crews record Bill Gibson's company line that an emotionally disturbed employee who had been drinking took over the plant at gunpoint, and that the situation had been "resolved." Kimberly grabs a microphone, breaks through the crowd, and asks pointed, angry questions of the company's operators, particularly of Ted Spindler who breaks down and speaks his mind: "He (Jack O'Dell) was the sanest man I ever met in my life. Jack O'Dell was a hero!" Kimberly weeps, and then gathering her emotions, says, "Let's just hope it doesn't end here." The film concludes with a commercial for microwave ovens runs alongside a screen showing the critical situation outside the Ventana Power Plant.

The China Syndrome

Character Identification

Draw a line from the character listed on the left to the description of that character on the right.

1. Don Jackovich   reporter of feature stories for KXLA-TV

2. Pete Martin   anchorman for KXLA-TV

3. Richard Adams   public relations person for the California Gas & Electric Company

4. Evan McCormack   owner of KXLA-TV

5. Ted Spindler   cameraman and film editor who is almost killed by thugs

6. Jack O'Dell   general manager of the Ventana Nuclear Power Plant

7. Kimberly Wells   manager of the television station, KXLA, in Los Angeles

8. Hector Sales   shift supervisor at Ventana Nuclear Power Plant

9. Mac Churchill   chairman of the board of California Gas & Electric Company

10. Bill Gibson   25-year company man who operates the control panel at the Ventana plant

11. Herman DeYoung   cameraman who steals a roll of film from the vault at KXLA-TV

Write the number of the character above next to the line of dialogue that he or she spoke. (Only 8 of the 11 characters are quoted.)

a. _____ "Let's just hope it doesn't end here."

b. _____ "It's totally irresponsible to go on the air without checking the facts."

c. _____ "I want you to keep the investigation on track, Herman. Let's get it over with.

d. _____ "You're a piece of talking furniture!"

e. _____ "Jack O'Dell wasn't a looney. He was the sanest man I ever met in my life."

f. _____ "The company's losing a half million dollars a day. Start 'er up, Jack!"

g. _____ "The system works. That's not the problem!"

h. _____ "A few minutes ago the situation inside was resolved."

The China Syndrome

Short Answer

1. Why is Kimberly Wells frustrated with her career as a news reporter for KXLA-TV?

_____

_____

2. What is the important detail at the Ventana "accident" of which Kimberly and Richard are unaware?

_____

_____

3. Why doesn't Kimberly help Richard get the film into the hands of another network when KXLA-TV suppresses the story?

_____

_____

4. What do you think Kimberly is feeling and thinking when Mr. Jackovich says, "Don't you worry your pretty head about it. Let us worry about that."

_____

_____

5. When does Kimberly actually break from doing entertaining stories to doing hard news?

_____

6. What does Kimberly learn from the experts who view the stolen film at Point Conception?

_____

_____

7. What does she learn from Jack O'Dell when she and Richard confront him about almost uncovering the core during the "accident"?

_____

_____

8. How does Kimberly act heroically in *The China Syndrome?*

_____

9. In what ways is Kimberly a "believable hero" rather than a one-dimensional superhero who challenges the bad guys and wins?

_____

10. In your opinion, what lies ahead for Kimberly Wells, reporter for KXLA-TV?

_____

_____

The China Syndrome

Interview

Using the information listed below, find a topic in your community or in your school that interests you—that makes you ask, "Why is that?" Then approach the topic from the perspective of an investigative reporter; ask the questions that fit the categories listed below. Make sure you have all the proper materials for conducting an interview, use the tips offered, write a strong lead (opening sentence) for your story, and include important quotes from major "players" in the story. Write it up and say it to the camera (video camcorder). Then play the tape for the class.

Section #1—The Five W's: Always get the basics into every news report:

WHO

WHAT

WHERE

WHEN

WHY

No one cares about great quotes and exciting lead sentences if they finish your report and don't know where the event took place, what happened, or who was there.

Section #2—Materials: Take along the following items:

1. **Notebook**—This should be big enough to write in, small enough to be easily carried and placed in your lap, and stiff-backed so you can write while holding it in your hand.

2. **Pen/pencils**—Take several with you on an interview. Stopping an interview to ask for a pen or pencil breaks the flow of conversation and can give the interviewee a chance to bring things to a dead stop.

3. **Tape recorder**—A microrecorder with a charged battery and new tape can work beautifully. A larger recorder can cause some people to "freeze up." It's best to tell the person that you need to tape the conversation, and then keep a microrecorder in your chest pocket or sticking inconspicuously out of a handbag.

4. **Camera**—You may miss some great moments if you rely solely on your memory. Take a small 35 mm camera—if possible, one that is fully automatic. A few snapshots of the area surrounding your interview will help you recall the atmosphere of the event. A photograph of an empty street after a story or of the remains of a burned school or hotel will bring back images, smells, sounds, and feelings that you might otherwise overlook or forget. A photograph helps capture impressions, the grist for any writer's mill.

Section #3—Tips: Keep in mind the following steps to ensure a quality interview:

1. Study your subject (person, place, or thing) long before you go for an interview. Check the local library, college library, state museum, local newspaper office, and neighbors, friends, and colleagues who might be able to give you any information that pertains to your subject.

2. Prepare a set of easily answered questions, even some "yes" or "no" questions with which to start the interview. Then make another list of tough, thought-provoking questions to finish with.

3. Ask for clarification. Have the interviewee restate his or her previous comment. For example, say, "I'm sorry. I don't quite understand." "Why do you think that is?"

4. Use silence as a tool. Silence can make the interviewee say something to fill the quiet space, which has become momentarily embarrassing. Listen when he or she starts talking at this point.

5. Note the surroundings. Make mental and written notes of the subject's movements, gestures, facial expressions, and tones of voice at various points during the interview.

The China Syndrome

Listening Exercise

In the movie *The China Syndrome* much technical information is given in a straightforward manner by "experts" in the field of nuclear power production. Yet even after hearing the statements made by these characters, it's difficult to understand exactly what is being said.

Below are two lengthy explanations given by the characters Jack O'Dell and Dr. Lowell, the scientist who explains the definition of "China Syndrome" to Kimberly Wells. Read one of the explanations to a partner. Then give your partner three minutes to write a summary of what you said. Next, listen as your partner reads the remaining explanation and write a summary of it in three minutes or less.

O'DELL: [at the Nuclear Regulatory Commission's investigation] A faulty relay in the generator circuit tripped the generator breakers open. The resultant transient in water level and pressure caused the turbine to trip and, for safety, relief valve number eight to open automatically. This does, of course, suddenly shut down the reactor—a "scram" situation.

NRC: Now reactor water level begins to drop.

O'DELL: Yes, but that's because we thought the water level was high; it turns out that the pen in the water level recorder was stuck.

NRC: So you began cutting off the feed water flow, releasing steam in the belief the water was too hot...

O'DELL: Yes, sir.

NRC: But in fact the water level was becoming dangerously low.

O'DELL: Low. Yes.

NRC: Why didn't your operator look at the other indicators?

O'DELL: I don't know. I was standing right beside him; I didn't look at it either.

DR. LOWELL: [explaining what could have happened during the "accident" at Ventana] If the core is exposed, the fuel heats beyond core heat tolerance in a matter of minutes. Nothing can stop it. And it melts right down through the bottom of the plant, theoretically to China; but of course as soon as it hits ground water it blasts into the atmosphere and sends out clouds of radioactivity. The number of people killed would depend on which way the wind was blowing. [It would] render an area the size of Pennsylvania permanently uninhabitable—not to mention the cancer that would show up later.

The China Syndrome

Answers

Character Identification

1. owner of KXLA-TV
2. anchorman for KXLA-TV
3. cameraman who steals a roll of film
4. chairman of the board
5. 25-year company man
6. shift supervisor
7. reporter of feature stories
8. cameraman and film editor
9. manager of television station
10. public relations person
11. general manager of the Ventana Nuclear Power Plant

    (a) 7   (b) 1   (c) 4   (d) 3   (e) 5   (f) 11   (g) 6   (h) 10

Short Answer

1. She wants to do serious news stories, not whimsical entertaining pieces.
2. Kimberly misses the small shudder that Jack O'Dell senses but can't immediately trace.
3. Kimberly wants to climb the ladder of success at KXLA and doesn't want to "rock the boat." Also, she believes Jackovich when he says their film of the plant is illegal.
4. She is insulted at his remarks because she is more than pretty; she's smart and talented.
5. She goes to hard news when she skips her whale story and travels to Point Conception to interview protestors.
6. She learns that the "China Syndrome" (uncovering the core) has been narrowly avoided.
7. She learns that many of the welds in the plant have not been X-rayed.
8. She enters the control room to conduct an intelligent interview with Jack O'Dell; she also gets the truth from Ted Spindler outside the power plant after Jack O'Dell has been killed.
9. Kimberly is believable because she *gradually* comes to the point where heroic action is required of her in order for truth to win out. She at first wants to be a good company person. She is afraid of losing her job, but eventually she risks it all to get to the truth.
10. (Possible response) Kimberly will become one of the best reporters in the city; if she should ever decide to leave Los Angeles, she will have her pick of reporting jobs.

Interview

Answers will vary.

Listening Exercise

Answers will vary.

THE CORN IS GREEN

Playwright: Emlyn Williams
Play Title: *The Corn Is Green*
Director: George Cukor

Running Time: 100 minutes
Year: 1979
Format: color

Summary

An elderly spinster, Miss Moffat, comes to a Welsh village in the late 1800's to establish a school for the children of the "common folk." What she finds is that many of her prospective students of age 12 and over are going down into the coal mines to work. In a telling opening scene Miss Moffat watches as a cage full of little boys, clean, innocent, and silent, is lowered into the depths of the deep, smoky shaft.

Her resolve is fixed. She organizes her meager staff: an elderly man named Jones and a mid-30's spinster named Miss Ronsbury. Miss Moffat's goal is to buy the barn next door from Sir Herbert Vasey, but the squire blocks her purchase, saying, "I'll have none of this nonsense in my village!" Miss Moffat calls him a "nincompoop" and walks off. Her anger vanishes upon returning home and reading an essay by a student, Morgan Evans. The work is powerful in its message and imagery. She calls Morgan in and asks if he'd like to know more. Morgan says, "I want to know what's behind all them books!"

The two begin a teacher-student relationship that lasts two full years before trouble starts. Morgan becomes restless under the yoke of his demanding tutor. He misses his old life, and he fears being teased and shunned. During this time, Moffat entreats the support of the squire to recommend Morgan for an Oxford scholarship.

Before she can tell Morgan the good news, he revolts and fights with her about the futility of his hard work. "What good will it do me in the mines?" Miss Moffat proceeds with her plans and says, "Be here tomorrow if you want to continue, or don't

come back." Later, at Miss Moffat's home, Morgan is alone with the maid's daughter, Bessie Watty. Bessie has a nasty streak and no morals and she lures the miserable Morgan to a one-night tryst from which she becomes pregnant.

On the day of the written entrance exam for Oxford, Bessie Watty returns from a stay in the city to announce that she is pregnant with Morgan's child. Miss Moffat keeps her away from Morgan who takes the exam and then travels by train to take the oral portion of the test. He is thrilled by the atmosphere at the college. It is a new life for him, a new world.

Days pass and the results finally arrive, along with Bessie Watty carrying a basket holding Morgan's baby son. Morgan has won the scholarship, but wants to refuse it in favor of doing his duty to the child and going to work in the mines to support him. Miss Moffat, realizing that Bessie wants only her freedom in the city, offers to adopt the baby so Morgan can continue his education at Oxford.

"We all walk in the dark, Morgan, and each of us must turn on his own light," Miss Moffat says. "You could be a man for us to be proud of." Morgan thanks her and decides to go to Oxford. The town rings the bell for a holiday and celebrates Morgan's good fortune.

In the last scene a boy runs to Miss Moffat's gate and asks if there will be school as usual tomorrow. "Yes there will be school the same as usual," she says, as the townsfolk carry Morgan off down the road on their shoulders, singing a Welsh song of victory and celebration.

The Corn Is Green

True or False and Multiple Choice

Mark the true statements below with a plus (+) and the false statements with a zero (0).

1. _____ The squire thought Miss Moffat was a man at first.

2. _____ Miss Moffat can be described as frail, and not too smart.

3. _____ The squire was a sexist aristocrat with no real occupation.

4. _____ The purpose of Miss Moffat's school was to get kids off the streets.

5. _____ Morgan Evans always knew he was capable of great things.

6. _____ Oxford gave Morgan a scholarship because they pitied him.

7. _____ Religion played a large role in Miss Moffat's school.

8. _____ Bessie Watty was kind but rather ignorant.

9. _____ Miss Moffat eventually realized she needed the squire's help.

10. _____ The squire eventually respected Miss Moffat for her hard work.

Write the letter of the correct answer on the line before each item.

11. _____ The squire thought that Miss Moffat was a colonel in the army because: (a) she sounded like a man in her letters (b) her nickname was "Little Colonel" (c) she signed her name L.C. Moffat (d) she kept excellent military records of her service in the nurses' corps

12. _____ Miss Moffat came to Wales because: (a) her uncle left her his house (b) her uncle left her his shares in the coal mine (c) she wanted to start a school (d) she was part of the Salvation Army which had a branch in Wales (e) a and b (f) a, b, and c (g) a, b, c, and d

13. _____ The title of the movie comes from: (a) an essay (b) a children's rhyme (c) a miner's song (d) the Bible

14. _____ Morgan Evans was: (a) a preacher's son (b) a miner's son (c) an orphan (d) a famous writer (e) a and b (f) b and c (g) c and d

15. _____ Bessie turned out to be selfish and unloving probably because: (a) she was uneducated as a child (b) she was poor in school (c) she was taught to be selfish (d) she was unloved by her mother (e) a and b (f) b and c

16. _____ Morgan rebels against Miss Moffat after two years because: (a) he's sick of the rigorous training (b) he misses his old friends (c) he hates being teased by his former buddies (d) he does not want to be beholden to Miss Moffat for his new opportunities in life (e) a and b (f) a, b, and c (g) a, b, c, and d (h) none of the above.

The Corn Is Green

Grammar: The Double Negative

In *The Corn Is Green,* Morgan Evans says at one point, "I don't want to see no Miss Moffat!" He's using a "double-negative;" the two negative words *don't* and *no* cancel each other out and drain the sentence of meaning. The sentence should read, "I don't want to see any Miss Moffat!"

Below are several sentences that are in the nonstandard, double-negative form. Rewrite them on the lines provided, leaving only one negative term in each sentence.

Example: "I don't have no reason to stay in this town!"
        Rewrite: "I have no reason to stay in this town!"
                or: "I don't have any reason to stay in this town!"

1. The squire couldn't hardly believe Miss Moffat was capable of hard work.

   _____

2. Morgan couldn't go nowhere without being teased about being Miss Moffat's "pet dog."

   _____

3. Morgan didn't have nothing going for him until he met Miss Moffat.

   _____

4. The squire hadn't no sense of what the villagers' lives were like.

   _____

5. Miss Moffat wouldn't take no "No's" for answers.

   _____

6. Don't nobody likes to be humiliated by others for being uneducated.

   _____

7. The townspeople couldn't hardly believe one of their own could win an Oxford scholarship.

   _____

8. When Morgan took the exam, Bessie wasn't nowhere around.

   _____

9. There's isn't no limit to what you can do with a good education.

   _____

10. There isn't nothing Miss Moffat would rather do than give others the gift of knowledge.

    _____

The Corn Is Green

Entrance Exam

When Morgan tried for the Oxford scholarship, he had to take a rigorous written and oral exam. Imagine that you are the director of admissions for an exclusive private high school. You need to create a test that will allow you to select only the best candidate for a $15,000 scholarship. On the lines below, write two questions in each category. Then, give the test to a small group of classmates to see how well they answer your questions. Grade the test and post the results. Who won the scholarship to your school? (You may want to administer part of the test orally, having the students stand and answer the questions aloud with no written notes.) Some key testing terms are: *Explain…Define…Summarize…Describe…Analyze…*

Literature

Question #1: _____

_____

Question #2: _____

_____

History

Question #1: _____

_____

Question #2: _____

_____

Science

Question #1: _____

_____

Question #2: _____

_____

Geography/Social Science

Question #1: _____

_____

Question #2: _____

_____

Name _____ Date _____

The Corn Is Green

Poetry

The poem below is by the great American poet Emily Dickinson. Read the poem and think about the questions that follow it. Then write a brief essay comparing what is expressed in the poem to Morgan Evans' life—how he was before, during, and after his time with Miss Moffat at the school.

He Ate and Drank the Precious Words

He ate and drank the precious words,
His spirit grew robust;
He knew no more that he was poor,
Nor that his frame was dust.

He danced along the dingy days,
And this bequest of wings
Was but a book. What liberty
A loosened spirit brings!

- How does one "eat" words?

- What is meant metaphorically by the phrase "drank the precious words?"

- How does one's spirit grow?

- In what ways did Morgan Evans's spirit grow?

- How was Morgan Evans a different person after learning? What did he learn about himself?

- How is a book like a set of wings?

- What "liberty" did Morgan feel?

_____

_____

_____

_____

_____

_____

_____

_____

_____

_____

_____

_____

_____

_____

The Corn Is Green

Answers

True or False and Multiple Choice

1. +	5. 0	9. +	13. a
2. 0	6. 0	10. +	14. f
3. +	7. 0	11. c	15. d
4. 0	8. 0	12. f	16. g

Grammar/The Double Negative

1. The Squire <u>couldn't believe</u> Miss Moffat was capable of hard work.
2. Morgan <u>could go nowhere</u> without being teased...
3. Morgan <u>had nothing</u> going for him...
4. The Squire <u>had no</u> sense of what the villagers' lives were like.
5. Miss Moffat <u>took no</u> "No's" for answers.
6. <u>Nobody</u> likes to be humiliated...
7. The townspeople <u>could hardly believe</u> one of their own could win...
8. When Morgan took the exam, Bessie <u>was nowhere</u> around.
9. There <u>is no limit</u> to what you can do with a good education.
10. There <u>is nothing</u> Miss Moffat would rather do than give...

Entrance Exam

Sample responses:

Literature

1. Analyze the role of nature in any three of Shakespeare's tragedies.
2. Define "Romanticism" and explain its origin and development in England before the American Revolution.

History

1. Describes the changes in politics, religion, and commerce in Great Britain after the Norman Conquest of 1066.
2. Summarize the effects of foreign policy of the United States on world affairs in the late nineteenth and early twentieth century.

Science

1. Summarize the significant contributions to scientific study of Galileo, Kepler, and Newton.
2. Describe the conflict between science and religion in Europe during the Age of Enlightenment.

Geography/Social Science

1. Define "geopolitics" and analyze its significance to the welfare and future of mankind.
2. Explain how the geography of China affects its position in and attitude toward the present global community.

Poetry

Answers will vary.

NEVER CRY WOLF

Author: Farley Mowat
Book Title: *Never Cry Wolf*
Director: Carroll Ballard

Running Time: 105 minutes
Year: 1983
Format: color

Summary

A young man named Tyler finds himself at the end of the Canadian railway line in a village called Nootzak, from where he will venture into the wilderness to do research on wolves, specifically on the killing habits of wolves who are suspected to be the cause of the demise of the caribou herd. Before he leaves, Tyler is told by a local man, "They will come after you son—just for the ugly fun of tearing you apart."

Terrified, but too concerned about being laughed at to turn back, Tyler engages a local gambler/bush pilot named Rosie Little to take him into the wilds. After attempting to take off three times and dumping most of the supplies out of the cargo door, Rosie heads the plane toward a vast, frozen, mountainous region 300 miles farther north where white Arctic wolves, Canis Lupus Arcticus, reside.

Tyler is shocked at the space, the silence, and the cold. Once on the ground he opens his supplies to find requisition forms, light bulbs, and several cases of frozen asparagus. He sits at his typewriter in the middle of a nameless, frozen lake and begins to type out a letter of complaint to the agency that dispatched him to such a forbidding place. Then he hears a howl. Dogs are coming toward him—several of them. He grabs a chunk of his dismantled bassoon as a weapon and hides under the canoe. An Eskimo approaches and guides Tyler to a boxlike shelter which becomes his laboratory. The Eskimo's name is Ootek. The wolf is Ootek's helping spirit.

After many days, Tyler sees the wolves. They are like ghosts in the fog of the Arctic spring. He tries to spy on them, but they simply circle around him and watch the goings-on. Then Tyler makes a bold move. He bangs and clatters his way to a spot where he sets up his tent, thus making himself conspicuous to the intelligent, suspicious wolves. They accept him, and Tyler after urinating around the two-acre perimeter of his "territory," gets down to the work of observing the wolves.

What he soon discovers is that there are no caribou in the Far North except during migration. In the meantime the wolves maintain their health and strength by eating mice. Realizing that no one would believe him, he begins a diet of mice for himself to see if a large carnivore could survive on such small rations. With 4,000 mice per acre, according to Tyler's calculations, there should be no lack of food supply.

One day Ootek returns with his son, Mike, a modern Eskimo, and observes the wolves along with Tyler. Ootek teaches Tyler much about wolf behavior and eventually reveals that he knows what the wolves are saying. One night the pack calls out that the caribou are coming—good hunting. Ootek and Tyler wait for the herd, and when it comes, Tyler observes the wolves killing a sick caribou. It is just as Ootek said—the wolves are a tool that nature uses to cut sickness from the herd.

But Tyler's reverie is soon shattered by the return of Rosie the bush pilot who has brought some rich clients with him to kill caribou and wolves. Tyler resists, and even shoots his shotgun toward Rosie's plane. Rosie flies off with a wolf's tail hanging from the plane's antenna. Tyler runs back to camp and realizes that George and Angeline, two wolves he's been observing for months, are dead. Mike awaits Tyler in camp and tells Tyler to get out because "This thing that's happening is too big for you."

Leaving with Ootek at the end of the film, Tyler says in narration, "I believe the wolves went off to a wild and distant place somewhere, but the truth is, I don't know."

Never Cry Wolf

Multiple Choice

Write the letter of the correct answer to each item on the line provided.

1. _____ Tyler goes to the Arctic region of Canada to: (a) test wolf habitat (b) find a pack of rare white Arctic wolves (c) find proof that the wolves are killing off the caribou (d) see if a large carnivore can sustain life by eating mice

2. _____ Tyler probably would have died within a short time if it hadn't been for: (a) Angeline and George (b) Ootek (c) Mike (d) Rosie (e) Uncle Albert (f) a and e (g) a, b, and e

3. _____ Canis Lupis means: (a) wolf (b) Eskimo (c) newcomer (d) prospector

4. _____ Most of the equipment supplied by the government for the Lupine Project was: (a) lost (b) traded for liquor (c) useless (d) broken (e) sold for wolf pelts

5. _____ Tyler's recurring nightmare is that: (a) he is left on an ice floe to die of starvation (b) he is chased off a cliff by a herd of caribou (c) he is devoured by a pack of wolves

6. _____ Rosie Little is a: (a) real estate speculator (b) gambler (c) research biologist (d) bush pilot (e) all of the above (f) a and b (g) a and c (h) a, b, and d (i) a, b, and c

7. _____ Tyler's success in observing the wolves is due to: (a) the wolves' patience and tolerance of him (b) Tyler's watchful, patient personality (c) Tyler's decision to make himself obvious to the wolves (d) Tyler's decision to move as close to the wolves as possible, rather than stay distant as the manual suggested (e) a and b (f) a, b, and d (g) a, b, and c (h) a, b, c, and d

8. _____ Tyler changes the "rules of the game" and makes a display of himself to the wolves on the premise that: (a) wolves are highly intelligent creatures (b) if he frightens them, the wolves will fear and respect him (c) we are suspicious of what we cannot see or understand

9. _____ Tyler eats mice for breakfast, lunch, and supper in order to substantiate his hypothesis that: (a) mice are plentiful: 4,000 per acre of Arctic tundra (b) mice are nutritious (c) a large carnivore can live well on mice (d) mice feed on small plants of the Arctic tundra

10. _____ Tyler's research dispelled the following myths about wolves: (a) wolves will attack, kill, and eat humans (b) wolves are nomads that live alone and apart from each other (c) wolves destroy herds of caribou (d) wolves hate people (e) a and b (f) a, b, and d (g) a, b, c, and d

11. _____ In the end, Tyler finds that the real devastation to the caribou herds has been caused by: (a) wolf packs (b) disease (c) Eskimo hunters (d) modern technology and civilization

12. _____ The title *Never Cry Wolf* was used to convey the message that: (a) wolves aren't always deadly killers (b) the government was claiming it had a problem with wolves when it really didn't (c) no one should underestimate the power of nature (d) a and c

Never Cry Wolf

Short Answer

1. Tyler says that he "jumped at the opportunity" to go the Canadian Arctic to study wolves. List his reasons.

   _____

   _____

   _____

2. Rosie Little says, "We're all prospectors, eh Tyler?" Explain what he means. How is Tyler a "prospector" when he first comes to the wilderness?

   _____

   _____

   _____

3. Why is Rosie more likable at the outset of the story than at the end?

   _____

   _____

   _____

4. In what ways are the Inuit Eskimos like the wolves of the Canadian Arctic?

   _____

   _____

   _____

5. Explain the metaphor "The wolf is a tool."

   _____

   _____

   _____

6. Tyler says he's always wanted to go to the wilderness to test himself against the evil lurking there. What evil does he find? How is this an irony?

   _____

   _____

   _____

7. At one point Tyler says, "I wished I could say thank you, straight into the universe." What has happened that has made Tyler so thankful?

   _____

   _____

   _____

Name _____   Date _____

Never Cry Wolf

Character Analysis

Find similarities between the two characters listed in each box below, and write these in the space provided. Then do the project outlined at the bottom of each page.

Ootek/Tyler	**Ootek/Mike**
Mike/Rosie	**Tyler/Rosie**

Project: Make a diagram similar to the one on this page. Then write your name, and the names of three acquaintances or friends, in *different pairs* for each of the four boxes. List some similarities between the people paired in each box. Whom are you most like? Unlike?

The Grapes of Wrath *and 24 More Videos*

Never Cry Wolf

Writing Activities

#1—The central conflict in the movie *Never Cry Wolf* is between modern civilization and the primitive world. In a two-page essay, tell what you believe is humanity's relationship to the natural world.How is the natural world different from human habitations? What is the obligation of humans to the natural world? What can modern people learn from the natural world? (Consider what Tyler learned from his experiences in the wild.)

#2—During the flight into the Arctic Rosie Little tells Tyler that the central problem of life is boredom: "Boredom, Tyler. Boredom. That's what's wrong!" Do you agree or disagree with Rosie? Define boredom and explain how boredom affects your life. What is the cure for boredom? Is adventure the cure? Where can one find adventure today?

#3—One of the most powerful forces portrayed in the film is silence. The vast sea of silence that engulfs Tyler eventually works to change the young biologist's view of life. What is Tyler's reaction to silence? What does he learn from it? Does he prefer it? Does the silence disturb him? Does silence disturb you? Explain.

#4—Set up an adventurous journey for yourself—an all-day trip to the city or to the country; a tour of three different malls or three different entertainment events (skating rink, dog track, bike trail, etc.); or an all-day tour of the place where your mom or dad works. Record your observations as Tyler did. Be precise. Record bits of dialogue spoken by people who may not even know you're listening. Record smells, sounds, and feelings that strike you throughout the day. Are there any conclusions you can draw about life in general from your experience? What did you learn about other people? About yourself? About the world you inhabit?

#5—The following Inuit Eskimo poem appears on the screen at the end of the film:

> *I think over again my small adventures, my fears.*
> *Those small ones that seemed so big, for all the vital things I had to get and to reach,*
> *And yet there is only one great thing, the only thing,*
> *To live to see the great day that dawns, the light that fills the world.*

Do you agree with the central premise of this poem? Explain.

#6—Write an additional segment to the film where Tyler is on the train heading back to the city. He's writing a final entry into his journal. What will he say about Ootek? About Mike? About Rosie and his "prospects" in the Arctic? What will Tyler promise himself as he makes his last notes about his experience in the wildest place he has ever known?

#7—Canadian author Farley Mowat (who wrote *Never Cry Wolf*) has written other fine books that are set in the natural world. Read some of these, and then write an essay that explores one central theme that seems to run through each of the books. Use quotes from the various books you read to support and develop your essay.

Never Cry Wolf

Answers

Multiple Choice

1. c	4. c	7. h	10. g
2. b	5. c	8. c	11. d
3. a	6. h	9. c	12. b

Short Answer

1. (a) He wanted to test himself against the evil lurking in the wilderness.
   (b) He wanted to find the basic animal he believed to be hidden within himself.

2. Rosie means that everybody is out to get something. Tyler's "treasure" was his quest for the truth about himself as much as it was to find about the wolves. Rosie is implying that Tyler is like all the rest of the white people in the Arctic, but Tyler proves him wrong.

3. Rosie has a sense of humor, adventure, and even joy at the beginning of the film. In the end he has lost his humor and is strictly business. A new coldness has come over him.

4. The Eskimos are trusting people who give folks room to prove their intentions; they live at one with nature, traveling with the seasons, taking shelter where they can; and like the wolves, they have no orphans in their culture.

5. The wolf is that creature which acts as a scalpel to cut the sickness from the herd; they kill only the sick and wounded caribou.

6. In the face of all the natural dangers that exist in the natural world, the worst, Tyler finds, is man. Rosie Little represents the most serious evil portrayed in the film.

7. Tyler has been brought to the outer edge of civilization and beyond, and there sees what life at its most basic can be. The challenge of living day to day excites and amazes him. His sense of childish wonder has been reawakened in him, and for this he is grateful.

Character Analysis

Ootek/Tyler: Ootek and Tyler share a sense of oneness with the natural world, represented by the wolves which have become their helping spirits. They have a spiritual responsibility toward the land and its creatures, much as priests would have.

Ootek/Mike: Ootek and Mike share the common heritage of the Arctic, both being from the same culture: Eskimo. They are also related by the code of the Eskimos in that Mike has been adopted by Ootek.

Mike/Rosie: Mike and Rosie share a bond of opportunism and materialism. They both want to get everything they can from the natural world, even if it means merchandising the products of the wild for their own conveniences.

Tyler/Rosie: Tyler and Rosie come from the white world where technology and modernization are a way of life. They are outsiders in a world that they were not born into. Both have deep connections to a system that lives outside of the natural environment of the Arctic. Both have a sense of what technology can do to a natural setting.

Writing Activities

Answers will vary.